To Lorne & Virginia
Smith

December 196
With Love
Dorothy Langley

Christmas Treasures

STORIES AND REMINISCENCES FROM GENERAL AUTHORITIES

Deseret Book Company
Salt Lake City, Utah

Cover illustration by Rebecca W. Hartvigsen

Hand lettering by John Gibby

Library of Congress Cataloging-in-Publication Data

Christmas treasures : stories and reminiscences from General
    Authorities.
        p.   cm.
    ISBN 0–87579–867–5
    1. Jesus Christ—Mormon interpretations. 2. Jesus Christ—
Nativity. 3. Christmas.
BX8643.J4C37   1994
232.92' 1—dc20   94–27612
                                                                         CIP

Printed in the United States of America

10 9 8 7 6 5 4 3 2 1

Contents

What Shall I Do Then with Jesus Which Is Called Christ?
President Gordon B. Hinckley 1

Christmas Giving and Receiving *Elder L. Tom Perry* 6

The Gift of Service *Elder John H. Groberg* 9

Our Christmas Lamb *Elder V. Dallas Merrell* 13

Christmas in the Holy Land *Elder M. Russell Ballard* 15

Lines of Christmas *Elder C. Max Caldwell* 19

The Least of These My Children *Elder Loren C. Dunn* 21

Christmas with Family *Elder Lino Alvarez* 25

The Greatest Gift *Elder Dallas N. Archibald* 27

Temple Blessings for Christmas *Elder Yoshihiko Kikuchi* 30

Christmas Thoughts of Home and of Prague *Elder Russell M. Nelson* 32

A Far Greater Gift *Elder James M. Paramore* 36

A Hong Kong Christmas *Elder Kwok Yuen Tai* 37

Christmas Experiences *Elder Earl C. Tingey* 39

Room in the Inn *Elder Neil L. Andersen* 41

Giving, Sharing, and Remembering *Elder Carlos E. Asay* 44

Christmas in the Mission Home *Elder LeGrand R. Curtis* 47

Merry Christmas, Murphy *Elder Stephen D. Nadauld* 49

Christmas Lessons *Elder Albert Choules Jr.* 53

The Best Christmas Ever *Elder Hugh W. Pinnock* 56

Christmas Riches during Lean Years *Elder Harold G. Hillam* 58

Christmas Giving *Elder Gene R. Cook* 62

Peace on Earth *Elder F. Burton Howard* 66

Our Last California Christmas *Elder John K. Carmack* 67

Lessons of True Sharing *Elder Lloyd P. George* 71

The Letters *Elder L. Lionel Kendrick* 74

The Real Christmas *Elder Richard P. Lindsay* 77

A Good Use for Fifty Dollars *Bishop H. David Burton* 79

A Christmas Gift of the Gospel *Elder Gary J. Coleman* 81

A Christmas Gift of Freedom *Elder Monte J. Brough* 83

The Help of the Lord *Elder J Ballard Washburn* 85

The Boy Who Sang *Elder F. Melvin Hammond* 87

"Silent Night, Holy Night" *Elder Joseph B. Wirthlin* 90

Christmas Blessings *Elder Robert E. Wells* 93

Christmas Memories *Elder Jack H Goaslind* 95

The Most Beautiful Christmas Tree *Elder Merlin R. Lybbert* 99

Sacrificing to Share *Elder L. Aldin Porter* 101

The Truth about Christmas *Elder Rex D. Pinegar* 103

Christmas Traditions in Mexico *Elder Horacio A. Tenorio* 105

Likening Luke 2 to Our Lives *Elder Jay E. Jensen* 109

Gratitude from Jerusalem *Elder Robert K. Dellenbach* 111

All Kinds of Christmases *Elder Rulon G. Craven* 113

Some Christmas Thoughts *Elder Joe J. Christensen* 115

The Gift of Life *Elder Malcolm S. Jeppsen* 117

Remembering *Elder Cree-L Kofford* 119

What Do You Mean, "No Room"? *Elder Graham W. Doxey* 123

Christmas: A Time of Hope *Elder Vaughn J. Featherstone* 126

Some Little Lessons from Christmas *Elder Spencer J. Condie* 130

The Child in the Manger *Elder Marvin J. Ashton* 134

The Joys of Christmas *President Ezra Taft Benson* 136

What Shall I Do Then with Jesus Which Is Called Christ?

PRESIDENT GORDON B. HINCKLEY

At this Christmas season, may I share a few thoughts concerning him whose birth we commemorate—the Man of Miracles, our Lord and Savior Jesus Christ. Although he healed the sick, raised the dead, caused the lame to walk, and made the blind to see, there is no miracle comparable to the miracle of Christ himself.

We live in a world of pomp and muscle, of strutting that glorifies jet thrust and far-flying warheads. It is the same kind of strutting that produced the misery of the days of Caesar, Genghis Khan, Napoleon, and Hitler. In this kind of world it is not easy to recognize that—

A babe born in a stable of the village of Bethlehem,

A boy reared as a carpenter of Nazareth,

A citizen of a conquered and subdued nation,

A man whose mortal footsteps never went beyond a radius of a hundred and fifty miles, who never spoke from a great pulpit,

who never owned a home, who traveled afoot and without purse Is actually the Creator of heaven and earth and all that in them are. Neither is it easy for many to recognize—

That he is the author of our salvation and his is the only name whereby we must be saved,

That he would bring light and understanding of things eternal and divine as none other has ever done,

That his teachings would not only influence the personal behavior of uncounted millions, but would also inspire political systems that dignify and protect the individual, and social truths that foster education and culture,

That his matchless example would become the greatest power for goodness and peace in all the world.

Truly, his coming, ministry, and place in our eyes is as foretold by the ancient prophet Isaiah: "For unto us a child is born, unto us a son is given: and the government shall be upon his shoulder: and his name shall be called Wonderful, Counsellor, The mighty God, The everlasting Father, The Prince of Peace." (Isaiah 9:6.)

I ask anew the question offered by Pilate two thousand years ago, "What shall I do then with Jesus which is called Christ?" (Matthew 27:22.) Indeed, we need continually to ask ourselves, What shall *we* do with Jesus who is called Christ? What shall we do with his teachings, and how can we make them an inseparable part of our lives? In light of these questions, at this season we ask another: What does Christmas really mean? May I suggest some things that it should mean?

Christmas means giving. The Father gave his Son, and the Son gave his life. Without giving there is no true Christmas, and without sacrifice there is no true worship. There is more to Christmas than neckties, earrings, toys, and all the tinseled stuff of which we make so much.

I recall an experience I heard at a stake conference in Idaho. A farm family in the community had just contracted for the installation of an additional and much-needed room on their home. Three or four days later the father came to the building-supply dealer and said, "Will it be all right with you if we cancel the contract? The bishop talked with John about a mission last night. We will need to set this room aside for a while." The building-supply dealer responded, "Your son will go on his mission, and he will find the needed room when he returns." Here was the spirit of Christmas—a family

sending a boy into the world to teach the gospel, and friends coming to help the family with their problems. What then, indeed, shall we do with Jesus who is called Christ?

Christmas means giving—and "the gift without the giver is bare." Giving of self, giving of substance, giving of heart and mind and strength in assisting those in need and in spreading the cause of His eternal truth—these are the very essence of the true spirit of Christmas.

Christmas means the Christ child, the babe wrapped in swaddling clothes, lying in a manger while angels sang and wise men traveled far to bring gifts. It is a beautiful and timeless story, and I hope each of us will read it again this season.

When I think of the Savior, I think not only of the words of Matthew and Luke, but also of the words of John: "In the beginning was the Word, and the Word was with God, and the Word was God.

"The same was in the beginning with God.

"All things were made by him; and without him was not any thing made that was made.

"In him was life; and the life was the light of men." (John 1:1–4.)

Here is something more than a babe in a manger; here is the Creator of all that is good and beautiful. I have looked at majestic mountains rising high against the blue sky and thought of Jesus, the Creator of heaven and earth. I have stood on the sand of an island in the Pacific and watched the dawn rise like thunder—a ball of gold surrounded by clouds of pink and white and purple—and thought of Jesus, the Word by whom all things were

2

made and without whom was not anything made that was made. I have seen a beautiful child—bright-eyed, innocent, loving, and trusting—and marveled at the majesty and miracle of creation. What then shall we do with Jesus who is called Christ?

This earth is his creation. When we make it ugly, we offend him. Our bodies are the work of our Creator. When we abuse them, we abuse him.

Christmas means eternity. As certainly as Christ came into the world, lived among men, laid down his life, and became the firstfruits of the resurrection, so, through that atonement, all become partakers of immortality. Death will come, but death has been robbed of its sting, and the grave of its victory. "I am the resurrection, and the life: he that believeth in me, though he were dead, yet shall he live: And whosoever liveth and believeth in me shall never die." (John 11:25–26.)

I remember standing before the bier of a young man whose life had been bright with hope and promise. He had been an athlete in his high school, and an excellent university student. He was a friendly, affable, brilliant young man. He had gone into the mission field. He and his companion were riding down the highway when a car, coming from the opposite direction, moved into their lane and crashed into them. He died in the hospital an hour later. As I stood at the pulpit and looked into the faces of his father and his mother, there came then into my heart a conviction that I had seldom before felt with such assurance. I knew with certainty, as I looked across

that casket, that this young man had not died, but had merely been transferred to another field of labor in the eternal ministry of the Lord.

Indeed, what shall one do with Jesus who is called Christ? Let us live with the certain knowledge that someday "we shall be brought to stand before God, knowing even as we know now, and have a bright recollection of all our guilt." (Alma 11:43.) Let us live today knowing that we shall live forever. Let us live with the conviction that whatever principle of intelligence and beauty and truth and goodness we make a part of our life here, it will rise with us in the resurrection.

Christmas means compassion and love and, most of all, forgiveness. "Behold the Lamb of God, which taketh away the sin of the world." (John 1:29.) How poor indeed would be our lives without the influence of his teachings and his matchless example. The lessons of the turning of the other cheek, the second mile traveled, the return of the prodigal, and scores of other incomparable teachings have filtered down the ages to become the catalyst to bring kindness and mercy out of much of man's inhumanity to man.

Brutality reigns where Christ is banished. Kindness and forbearance govern where Christ is recognized and his teachings are followed.

What shall we do then with Jesus who is called Christ? "He hath shewed thee, O man, what is good; and what doth the Lord require of thee, but to do justly, and to love mercy, and to walk humbly with thy God?" (Micah 6:8.)

"Wherefore, I say unto you, that ye

ought to forgive one another; for he that forgiveth not his brother his trespasses standeth condemned before the Lord; for there remaineth in him the greater sin." (D&C 64:9.)

Christmas means peace. I remember being in Europe a number of years ago at the time tanks were rolling down the streets of a great city, and students were being slaughtered with machine-gun fire. I stood that December day in the railroad station in Berne, Switzerland. At eleven o'clock in the morning, every church bell in Switzerland began to ring, and at the conclusion of that ringing every vehicle stopped—every car on the highway, every bus, every railroad train. The great, cavernous railway station became deathly still. I looked out the front door across the plaza. Men working on the hotel opposite stood on the scaffolding with bared heads. Every bicycle stopped. Every man and woman and child dismounted and stood with bared, bowed heads. Then, after three minutes of prayerful silence, trucks, great convoys of them, began to roll from Geneva and Berne and Basel and Zurich toward the suffering nation to the east, laden with supplies—food, clothing, and medicine. The gates of Switzerland were thrown open to refugees.

As I stood there that December morning, I marveled at the miraculous contrast between the oppressive power mowing down students in one nation and the spirit of a Christian people in another who bowed their heads in prayer and reverence, then rolled up their sleeves to provide succor and salvation.

What shall we do then with Jesus which is called Christ? "For I was an hungred, and ye gave me meat: I was thirsty, and ye gave me drink: I was a stranger, and ye took me in: naked, and ye clothed me: I was sick, and ye visited me: I was in prison, and ye came unto me." (Matthew 25:35-36.)

He whose birth we commemorate this season is more than the symbol of a holiday. He is the Son of God, the Creator of the earth, the Jehovah of the Old Testament, the fulfillment of the Law of Moses, the Redeemer of mankind, the King of Kings, the Prince of Peace.

I thank our Eternal Father that mankind in these latter days has been so blessed to know of Christ with added certainty and added knowledge. I rejoice with thanksgiving that he has reaffirmed his matchless gospel truths in their fullness, and that he has restored his priesthood power and church to prepare a people and make ready for his eventual coming in great glory and power in the opening of the millennial era.

I rejoice at Christmastime that as a people, we Latter-day Saints know of his existence and reality, and receive certain direction from him.

"And now, after the many testimonies which have been given of him, this is the testimony, last of all, which we give of him: That he lives!

"For we saw him, even on the right hand of God; and we heard the voice bearing record that he is the Only Begotten of the Father—

"That by him, and through him, and of him, the worlds are and were created, and the inhabitants thereof are begotten sons and daughters unto God." (D&C 76:22–24.)

This is our testimony to all mankind. It is our gift and blessing to the world. He is our joy and our salvation, and we will find Christmas of greater meaning in our own lives as we share these truths with others.

What shall we do with Jesus who is called Christ?

Learn of him. Search the scriptures, for they are they which testify of him. Ponder the miracle of his life and mission. Try a little more diligently to follow his example and observe his teachings. Bring the Christ back into Christmas.

This chapter was adapted from "What Shall I Do Then with Jesus Which Is Called Christ?" *Ensign*, December 1983. © The Church of Jesus Christ of Latter-day Saints. Used by permission.

Christmas Giving and Receiving

ELDER L. TOM PERRY

The Christmas season has always been a special time for me, as I suppose it is for most of us. I was reared in a family that believed in making Christmas the most joyous season of the year. As my father was the bishop during the first eighteen years of my life, our celebration included not only the family, but the ward and community as well. Christmas Eve was a memorable time as we held what would be called today a Christmas family home evening. It always concluded with our father reading the account of the birth of the Savior from Matthew and Luke.

Father delighted in surprising us during our celebration at home. His creative mind worked overtime to bring a new experience for us at Christmastime. Unexpected happenings often occurred. For example, one year Santa Claus had difficulty getting down our chimney. Some of our toys fell from his bag as he was making his descent. On Christmas morning we found the number of presents greatly reduced, with a big note from dear old Santa pinned to our Christmas tree, explaining what had

happened. He said that he was too rushed to attempt to find the missing toys, but perhaps if we searched the house they could be found. Of course, we conducted a thorough search. The lost toys were finally found in front of the doors of the furnace in our basement.

Father wanted each ward member to enjoy the Christmas spirit. Activities were planned to assist each age group. The cultural hall was beautifully decorated, making each occasion more festive. In addition, a big Christmas party was held there each year for the entire ward. I have many fond memories of these special events.

I don't believe any family in our ward ever missed having all the ingredients necessary for a delicious Christmas dinner. I was accustomed to pulling my little, red wagon around the ward, following along behind my father, taking Christmas baskets to those in need. The baskets were prepared carefully by the Relief Society sisters, and all ward members who could, made contributions to their contents.

Our community of Logan, Utah,

made each Christmas season a special time. Beautifully lighted trees lined Main Street. Tabernacle Square, ablaze with Christmas lights, was the center of all the activities of the community. Beautiful choirs performed concerts of Christmas music every weekend from Thanksgiving until Christmas. The culminating event was a Christmas pageant held in the Tabernacle on Christmas morning, as I remember, at 7:00 A.M. It was a wonderful way to start the day before going home to our own Christmas activities.

After we were married, my wife and I decided to create our own Christmas traditions. We moved every few years, so we determined that we would stay at home for Christmas and not try to return to the homes of our parents, as much as we would have liked to.

It is difficult to build Christmas traditions for your family when your profession is in the retail business, for the period between Thanksgiving and New Year's is the major selling season. I would work from twelve to fifteen hours per day, Monday through Saturday each week. Because I was spending so much time at the store, we had to build our traditions around store activities. These included accepting calls to Santa, listening to the special choirs that visited our stores, driving to see the Christmas lights as we traveled between the various store branches, and assisting the community in bringing Christmas to needy families.

Our moves had taken us from Utah to Idaho to Washington to California to New York to Massachusetts. We had moved from the small communities to the large, from the moderate climates to

the bitter cold. Each location enlarged our Christmas experience, and each was unique in its ways of celebrating Christmas. Our moves ended when I was called to be a General Authority at the October general conference in 1972. At the time of the call, the First Presidency counseled me to do everything I could to separate myself from my employment with good feelings. My employers requested that I stay as long as I could into the Christmas season, so I agreed to remain there until almost Christmastime. We left ourselves just enough time to drive from Boston to Salt Lake.

Delayed by snow, we arrived in Salt Lake just two days before the Christmas celebration. Nothing we owned, except that which we carried with us, arrived in Utah until after Christmas. By the time we found an apartment to rent, it was too late to even think about celebrating, so we decided to just miss Christmas that year.

Elder Marion D. Hanks heard of our arrival and our plans to bypass Christmas. He insisted that we come to his home and spend Christmas Eve with his family and other invited guests needing a Christmas celebration.

I was a little uncomfortable with the arrangement at first. From the time of my boyhood I had helped Dad deliver baskets to the needy at Christmastime. My business experience had always found us in the act of making Christmas special for someone else. This was the first time I had ever found myself in the position of having to receive this loving care from others. It placed Christmas in a whole different light.

We had a delightful evening with the Hanks family on Christmas Eve. We sang carols, read scriptures, discussed Christmases past, and enjoyed delicious food. As we prepared to leave Elder and Sister Hanks's home and return to our apartment, they presented us with a small, decorated Christmas tree. We returned to our little apartment, placed the Christmas tree in the center of the room, and had a wonderful family discussion about what it means not only to be a generous giver, but also to be a gracious receiver.

This Christmas experience caused an awakening in my soul of the real meaning of Christmas and why we celebrate this greatest of all birthdays. We are the recipients of the most wonderful blessings it is possible for mankind to receive, including the gift of immortality, through the atoning sacrifice of our Lord and Savior. We also have the wonderful promise of life eternal, which is the greatest of all God's gifts to mankind, if we will only qualify ourselves to receive it. The gift is there waiting to be opened, depending upon our obedience to the plan the Lord established for us from the very beginning. As this particular Christmas ended, I found myself pondering this marvelous blessing, and my heart was filled with gratitude.

This is one of the Christmases I will always remember, especially for the joy it brought into my life, and for the renewed testimony of the mission of the Savior and his gift to all mankind.

The Gift of Service

ELDER JOHN H. GROBERG

December is warm in Tonga, where I spent several Christmases as a young missionary in the 1950s. Despite the hot, humid weather, the Christmas spirit is beautiful. What a blessing it is when people think more about others and less about themselves!

There was not a lot of physical gift-giving in Tonga, as there were not a lot of things to give. People were poor in terms of worldly possessions, but they gave marvelous gifts of love, service, and kindness. During the warm evenings around Christmas, many singing groups and bands went around serenading. Even with the oppressive heat the feeling of peace and good cheer seemed to permeate everything.

A few months before Christmas one year we had been asked to raise £500 so we could start building a new brick chapel in Pangai. We made an assessment of £50 each to ten separate families, with the request that they have the money in by January 1. Most of the families had completed their allotment, but one older couple was still struggling. They were a faithful grandparent couple whose children were all married and gone.

The grandfather originally had some sources in mind where he could get the money, but one by one those sources failed, and he realized he would need to go to his plantation on another island and make copra to sell. (Copra is used commercially for soaps and oils.) Making copra involved gathering coconuts, cutting them open, extracting the meat, drying it in the sun, and selling it to the *mataka* (copra board) to get the needed money. He was determined to meet the January 1 deadline, so two weeks before Christmas he left for his plantation.

Shortly after he left, a nine-year-old granddaughter came from Tongatapu to spend the holidays. Her arrival was unannounced, but welcomed by her grandmother.

The grandmother and her granddaughter had a good time together, but a few days before Christmas the granddaughter became very ill with a high fever. Even though her grandmother put her to bed and cared for her well, the fever seemed to get worse. The grandmother asked my companion and me to administer to the girl, which we did. I felt she would be all right and we continued about our other activities.

The day before Christmas, one of the missionary schoolteachers and I visited several families to wish them the season's best. As we concluded our visits, I asked my companion where else he thought we should go that Christmas Eve. He replied, "I've heard that the granddaughter is still doing poorly and that the grandfather has not yet returned. I'm sure the grandmother is very tired from the constant care she has been giving her granddaughter. Why don't we go to her house and volunteer to watch her granddaughter tonight and let her get some rest?"

What a great idea! I thought. *Why don't I think of things like that?*

It was early evening when we arrived at the grandmother's house and explained what we proposed to do. Seldom have I seen more grateful eyes or felt more sincere appreciation. The grandmother looked at us a long time, probably studying our seriousness, and then said, "She is very ill. I have been up day and night with her for the last three days. I am very tired, and I'm not sure I can make it another night. Thank you. Thank you! I have been using this cloth and bowl of water to cool her brow and this woven fan to give her some air movement. She has not talked at all the last few days, only moaned. I'm not sure if she will get well or not. Maybe I should try to stay up and help."

My companion said, "No, you go and rest. *Kolipoki* (my Tongan name) and I

will fan her and cool her forehead, and she will be all right. Now run along and sleep." She looked at us again for a long time, then left. I imagine she was asleep the second she got to her room.

We were on the front veranda of the house, where it was a little cooler than inside. We immediately started fanning the granddaughter and cooling her forehead with the wet cloth. She seemed in a bad way. Her breathing was strange, her fever was high, her eyes were closed, and her moans were pathetic. We devised a system whereby one would hold the wet cloth and the other would fan the air through it to get some cool air moving around the girl's mouth and head.

It doesn't sound like much work, but the anxiety of the situation, the sultry evening, and the exertion to get water, rinse the cloth, and constantly wave the fan caused us both to tire quickly. I appreciated the grandmother and her constant care more than ever.

At around eleven o'clock we realized we must do something different to make it through the night, as we were both very tired. My companion again came up with an idea. "Why don't we take turns?" he said. "You sleep for an hour while I care for her, then I'll wake you and you care for her an hour while I sleep, then you wake me, and so on. At least we'll get through the night that way."

"Fine," I said. "Who should start?"

"I'll start," he replied. "You rest first." So I lay down and he started caring for the child alone. At midnight he woke me and I fanned with one hand and sponged her forehead with the other until one o'clock, when I woke him. He woke me at two and I, in turn, woke him at three. I knew he would wake me for my next turn at four o'clock. Even though I was very tired, I knew this was fair.

The next thing I knew, sunlight was streaming into my eyes. I awakened, jumped up, and said, "What time is it?"

"It's six o'clock," my companion replied.

"Six o'clock! You were supposed to get me up at four! Why didn't you wake me?" I asked.

He had a broad smile on his face, which was intensified by the bright rays of the early morning sun. That smile seemed to come from deep within his soul; it encompassed his whole being as he replied, "Oh, you looked so tired. I decided to let you sleep. It's my present to you. Merry Christmas!"

I couldn't say anything. I just looked at him in admiration and wondered, *Why don't I think of things like that? My companion is a great man. God loves him. He stayed up for me. Why am I so weak?* I thought of the Savior coming to his sleeping disciples and asking, "Could ye not watch with me one hour?" (Matthew 26:40.) The Savior stayed up most of the night performing the greatest work of love in the world while those close to him slept. Yet, as he returned and saw them sleeping again, he merely looked at them and quietly said, "Sleep on."

I felt ashamed, yet I also felt happy as I saw the joy in my companion's face. His radiant smile was almost angelic.

Sometime during those early morning hours the girl's moaning ceased and her fever broke. She stirred and opened her eyes. Although she was still very weak, we knew she would be all right. We waited till midmorning, then knocked on the door to wake the grandmother. She answered the knock quickly, possibly expecting the worst. When she came out on the porch, her granddaughter was sitting up. We were all smiles as we said in unison, "Merry Christmas!" It was good to have her and her granddaughter both feeling so much better—a wonderful way to start Christmas Day. We had many other things to do, so we left and went about our regular missionary activities.

Over time I largely forgot about this experience until many years later when I was asked to speak at the funeral for my faithful Tongan missionary companion. He had lived a good life and had died of cancer. While speaking in Tongan, I suddenly received a flash of understanding that made a deep and clear impression on me. I emphasize that this was not a vision, a revelation, or a dream, but rather a feeling and an understanding wherein I sensed the following:

I saw a beautiful place with throngs of people anxiously waiting to get to a certain area. There was no pushing or shoving, but rather a respectful and excited pressing forward to this particular place.

I saw a young man in the throng smiling and patiently moving along with the others when suddenly his name was called and someone in authority came and took him by the arm and led him past the waiting crowds, directly to the desired area. His guide said a few words to someone who seemed to control the entrance, and this person smiled and ushered the young man through.

Everyone in the huge crowd seemed to be aware of what had happened. People turned to one another and began to comment, not in anger or jealousy but rather in wonder and happiness for the young man who had gotten to that desirable place so quickly.

The guide came back and began waiting patiently with the throngs of people. Someone leaned over and asked him about the young man. The guide whispered something to him and immediately the questioner's face lit up with a deep smile. He nodded his head approvingly and turned and told his neighbor. Almost instantly everyone seemed to know the answer. I strained to understand and finally heard someone say, "Oh, he let his companion sleep when he was very tired."

I offer no more explanation than what I have related. I learned that deeds of sacrifice, deeds of selflessness and honesty, deeds of effort in sincerely trying to help others, especially at the expense of one's own comfort, never go unnoticed by the powers of heaven.

This chapter appeared originally in John H. Groberg, *In the Eye of the Storm* (Salt Lake City: Bookcraft, Inc., 1993), pp. 236–40. Used by permission.

Our Christmas Lamb

ELDER V. DALLAS MERRELL

In 1965 we were enrolled in graduate school at the University of Southern California and living in Inglewood, California, with our five young children. On Christmas Day that year our two-month-old baby died of sudden infant death syndrome, or crib death.

We knew that this daughter, Mary, would be ours forever, provided we were worthy. That knowledge was a great comfort to us from the moment of her sudden and unexpected death. But after we had recovered from the shock of her loss, my wife, Karen, still could not rid herself of the sorrow she felt. She grieved that the older children were too young to remember their departed baby sister and that neither set of grandparents had even seen her. Mary seemed destined to have lived and died to be remembered only by her parents.

This concern became the burden of Karen's prayers. Eventually an idea began to form in her mind. She felt strongly that if, through Mary's death, she and the baby could work together to change someone's life, the comfort she

needed so much would come. Her search for that special someone began.

In late January, when Karen went to get her hair cut, the stylist, Jan, inquired about the baby. When she learned about Mary's death, Jan asked: "Was your baby baptized before she died?" Karen explained our belief that infants do not need baptism, but that they are innocent until the age of accountability.

Jan told Karen that her father had been a young child in his family when their baby died, and he remembered the local minister of their church telling his grieving parents that they could not bury the baby in the church cemetery because it had not been baptized. Her father, even as young as he was, decided he would never again set foot in the door of that church or any other church that taught such doctrine. And he never did.

Karen could hardly believe what she was hearing. Could this be the person she was praying to find? She asked Jan if she would like to have the missionaries come and teach her about our church. To her great joy, Jan said she would. Three months later she was baptized. That was the day Karen began to feel peace about Mary's death. Together, with the Lord's help, mother and child had found someone within the circle of their influence who could be touched by the child's death. Mary had left her mark. Now Karen was content.

Christmas for us is a bittersweet day. We miss our daughter. But the pain has greatly diminished as we have focused on our feelings of gratitude for the Savior's birth, for his profound atonement, and for the universal resurrection, which assures us that we will see our precious child again. No greater gift could come to us.

A friend shared with us a poem that described the Savior leading a flock of sheep. When he came to the edge of a river, he waded in, but the sheep were afraid to follow. So, coming back to the shore, he gently gathered a little lamb into his arms and waded out again. This time the mother of the lamb followed him and behind her came the rest of the flock, until they were all safely on the opposite shore.

Mary is a beacon light—drawing us, through the power of our shared love, to her celestial home. Like the mother sheep who follows her lamb, we find renewed courage to forge through the dangerous waters of earth life. And on that distant shore, we see not just our own little lamb, but the Shepherd himself, waiting patiently for each of us to join them.

Christmas in the Holy Land

ELDER M. RUSSELL BALLARD

For centuries, faithful Jews scattered throughout the world have offered a simple Passover prayer reflecting respect for their heritage and longing for their ancestral home. For as long as I can remember, I expressed a similar sentiment around our home at Christmastime. "Wouldn't it be great," I said every year for several decades to my wife, Barbara, "if just once our whole family could celebrate the birth of the Savior together in the Holy Land."

"It would be wonderful," Barbara always agreed, "but our children all have young families with lots of expenses. It will probably be a while before everyone can afford to make such a trip." She was right, of course, but I could never shake the dream that was rekindled every time we took the Christmas decorations out of storage and began our annual holiday preparations.

"Maybe next year we will be getting ready to go to the Holy Land," I would say hopefully, amid the stringing of lights and the hanging of tinsel.

"Maybe," Barbara would reply. But something in her voice implied that she was looking down a road that might take our family a long time to travel.

Meanwhile, on two occasions Barbara and I had visited the Holy Land on Church assignments. We loved the unique and very tender feelings we had while traveling in the land where Jesus lived. We felt that our experiences there drew us closer to him.

After our second trip to Israel several years ago, my desire to share its sights and sounds and feelings with my children became so intense that I decided we couldn't wait for the children to be able to afford the trip. Barbara and I determined to find a way to save the money to take our children and their companions with us to the Holy Land.

On December 3, 1993, our dream became a reality when Barbara and I and our seven children and their spouses arrived at Ben Gurion Airport in Tel Aviv. We left the airport on the bus that we had hired to carry the family on a six-day tour of the Holy Land. As we approached Jerusalem, I realized that our saving for this trip over the years was one of the most important investments that Barbara and I would ever make. The feeling of excitement that radiated from our children was sure evidence that our decision to visit the Holy Land together near Christmastime would be a transcendent experience for all of us.

Since being ordained an Apostle over eight years ago, I have had the strong desire that my family should walk with me in the Holy Land so I could teach them about Jesus and share with them my sure witness that he is, in fact, the Son of the Living God, our Savior and our Redeemer. Our trip lived up to my expectations. We had some extraordinary experiences during the six days we spent there together.

With the able help of Mike and Pam Bawden as our personal guides, we traced the Savior's footsteps, scriptures in hand, and felt the spirit of His mortal ministry. We went from Jerusalem to Jericho, through the Jordan Valley to Tiberius. We took a boat ride on the Sea of Galilee, visited Capernaum, and had a wonderful experience reading the Sermon on the Mount right there on the Mount of Beatitudes. Each event touched our hearts deeply and increased our love for the Savior.

Our visit to Mount Tabor, where President Spencer W. Kimball said he felt that the Transfiguration took place, was an experience never to be forgotten. From Mount Tabor, our bus moved us toward Nazareth. There we read the story of Mary and Joseph. This was the beginning for us of reliving the wondrous events we celebrate every Christmas.

"And in the sixth month the angel Gabriel was sent from God unto a city of Galilee, named Nazareth,

"To a virgin espoused to a man whose name was Joseph, of the house of David; and the virgin's name was Mary.

"And the angel came in unto her, and said, Hail, thou that art highly favoured, the Lord is with thee: blessed art thou among women.

"And when she saw him, she was troubled at his saying, and cast in her mind what manner of salutation this should be.

"And the angel said unto her, Fear not, Mary: for thou hast found favour with God.

"And, behold, thou shalt conceive in thy womb, and bring forth a son, and shalt call his name JESUS.

"He shall be great, and shall be called the Son of the Highest: and the Lord God shall give unto him the throne of his father David." (Luke 1:26–32.)

These passages of scripture had ever so much impact as we walked the streets of Nazareth and imagined all that Mary had experienced.

From Nazareth, we continued traveling east and south over the hills of Samaria to Caesarea. Finally, after two days on the bus, we drove through Samaria back to Jerusalem.

On December 7, early in the morning, we stood on the balcony at the Jerusalem Center and looked at models representing four different time periods of the Old City. Our family was becoming comfortable in the Holy Land. We left the Center and took our journey to Bethlehem, where the beautiful Christmas story continued to unfold. Once again, being in that holy place near the sacred spot of the Savior's birth made our reading of the events more poignant and personal than any of us could remember.

From Bethlehem we traveled about three miles east to Shepherds' Field, where we enjoyed a wonderful view looking across the rocky valley back to the Savior's birthplace. We walked by a Bedouin camp, and a beautiful little Bedouin girl came out and followed us.

Brother Bawden told us that the star, from that shepherds' vantage point, must have trailed a shaft of light that fell over the spot where the manger was. From where we sat, we could clearly see the Church of the Nativity. In this place we read Luke 2:1–20 and Matthew 2:1–12 together.

As we absorbed all that was before us, the afternoon grew blustery and cold. We lingered, though, wanting to stay as long as possible to enjoy the view and ponder the significance of where we were. A Bedouin shepherd with his foreign-looking flock of dark, brown-faced, long-eared sheep came up out of the valley and appeared over the hill. As he began guiding his flock toward us, a profound feeling swept over us all. A timelessness engulfed us as we realized that we were witnessing a scene that had been repeated over and over for millennia. We thought of the shepherds on that holy night who followed the shaft of light that shone down from the star. We pictured in our minds what it might have been like to enter the cave and feel the sense of reverence and awe that would have prevailed there.

Our thoughts turned to the Christ child, the Good Shepherd. We talked about how beautiful, sweet, and tender he must have been, how soft his downy cheek must have felt against Mary's. Our hearts were filled with deep gratitude toward the precious baby Jesus of long ago. Our knowledge was strengthened immeasurably that, because of Christ, we can live together as an eternal family if we strive diligently to follow his teachings and live as he has asked us to. It wasn't as though we didn't understand this already, but somehow at this moment we knew it to be true like never before. This was a binding moment for us as a family.

This special day concluded where it had started, back at the Jerusalem Center, where we gathered in the beautiful auditorium. Two of our dear friends and neighbors, Judy and Tom Parker, who were serving as missionaries at the Center, joined us. Sister Parker played the organ for us, and we sang the songs of Christmas together as a family. The carols seemed especially meaningful as we sang while looking through the massive windows that give a panoramic view of the Holy City.

Never before had we sung "Joy to the World," "Oh, Come, All Ye Faithful," "Angels We Have Heard on High," "Silent Night," "Away in a Manger," "It Came upon the Midnight Clear," "O Little Town of Bethlehem," "While Shepherds Watched Their Flocks," and "Far, Far Away on Judea's Plains" with as much meaning as when we sang these Christmas carols with the view of the Old City before our eyes. What a glorious celebration this was for each of us!

When the time came for us to leave the Holy Land and we boarded our plane for the flight back to the United States, we were different as individuals and as a family because the life and ministry of our Lord Jesus Christ had touched our minds and hearts in a new, penetrating way. The life and mission of the Redeemer, the Good Shepherd of us all, were more permanently etched in our souls than ever before. Barbara and I knew that we had celebrated Christmas with our family in the most important and meaningful way possible.

Lines of Christmas

ELDER C. MAX CALDWELL

My travels as a member of the Europe Area Presidency have taken me throughout many lands previously under Communist domination and control. In one region, fruits of long-standing imposed atheism and controlled religious behavior and expression were conspicuous. I could not help but notice the marked contrast of countenance between the few who basked in the gospel light and the masses who yet remained in spiritual darkness. So many did not appear to be happy; they did not smile. Their association with each other seemed to be based on doubt or mistrust. In some places, there was an air of callousness in crowds and indifference in individuals. A sense of community or common effort was difficult to find. Here I experienced a particularly memorable Christmas season.

In this region many people stood in lines, waiting not to buy Christmas presents, but to try to buy bread or milk or some other basic commodity. One missionary said that when he first arrived, he and his companion would get in a line whenever they saw one. While one held a place, the other would inquire why the people were waiting. Because the missionaries always needed food of some kind, they would wait, hoping to obtain the item being offered at that location. Meanwhile, they talked to the people in the line about the restored gospel and shared their testimonies with those who would listen. And some did.

One night during my trip, I had an unusual dream. I could clearly see a long line of people waiting their turn to obtain food. My attention was drawn to a lady in the line whose arms were outstretched in front of her. In her arms was a little boy, about two years old, lying on his back. His arms and legs fell limply and his head drooped down. No words were spoken, but I understood that the little boy was dead, that he had died while his mother stood waiting in line for food to feed him. The vivid reality of that dream has indelibly stamped in my memory the desperation I discerned in those people. They stand in lines with hope of survival.

Many lack other things that could make life more comfortable and provide temporal relief, things for which there are no lines. It is not uncommon for people to live without electricity and heat, for example. They know the discomforts of darkness and cold all too well.

I met a man whose country had gone through a civil revolution. He had experienced arrests, torture, and physical privation of many kinds although he was innocent of any wrongdoing before his country's law. However, somebody had suspected and accused him. He was forced into a lineup against a wall in front of a firing squad. As his group awaited execution, new orders were received and this line of men was freed.

Along with his fellow citizens he, too, had stood in many food lines. He told of waiting hours in line, only to hear the shopkeeper say there was only enough left for three, or four, or five more people, narrowly not enough for him.

Then the missionaries found him. There were no lines in the Church; all were welcome and free to choose. And he did choose the spiritual and eternal gifts that have been freely offered. To receive, he needed only to trust the Giver and His written lines, which require an investment not in time only, but in faith: "Whosoever believeth in him should not perish." (John 3:16.)

I also learned of one woman who received the discussions from the missionaries and the witness of the Spirit from the Lord. She expressed her desire to be baptized, and arrangements were made for the service. As the font was being filled, the water heater was discovered to be broken. The water was the temperature of the wintry cold pipes that conveyed it. She was told of the problem and that the baptism would need to be postponed until repairs could be made. Of course, no one knew how long the delay would be, because repair parts were in short supply and hard to obtain. She was not disappointed; she was determined; she would not be denied, and her baptism took place. She endured and survived the cold that she might not perish.

During my trip, I also attended church meetings in one of the developing countries and sang with the Saints from their small songbook, a limited selection of hymns that have been translated into their native language. We sang together a familiar hymn, "Because I Have Been Given Much." I wept as I thought what these people were offering in a song of the righteous, ascending unto the Lord as a prayer unto him. They do not possess many tangible, temporal, and temporary things. Even so, they still share with and help one another in many ways. Their offerings are significant and meaningful. These faithful souls have been given much of the unseen, spiritual, and eternal treasure. The warmth of the Spirit, the light of the gospel, and the nourishment of words of eternal life sustain them.

As I returned to our warm and comfortable apartment, I did not care that we had only a small Christmas tree with miniature lights sitting on the window ledge. I did not even notice the absence of the usual abundance of gifts beneath the tree. But I was acutely aware that I, too, have been given much. I am grateful for the comfort of these eternal Christmas lines, "I am . . . the light and the life of the world—a light that shineth in darkness." (D&C 45:7.)

The Least of These My Children

ELDER LOREN C. DUNN

Memories of Christmas past for me center not on one Christmas but on experiences that were parts of many Christmases.

Growing up in a small town provides many such memories. Christmas was centered in family, neighborhood, church, and school. It was a busy time of year for us because we were in the newspaper business, and the Christmas season meant a larger newspaper with Christmas stories and advertising. Christmas Day was a day of much-needed rest for my father, and while we children were up at the crack of dawn, he and Mother joined in a little later, having laid out Christmas for us the night before.

As children we had a careful ritual to follow. Whoever woke first would wake the others, because we would always go together into the front room where the tree and gifts were. We brushed our teeth and had breakfast first, which was our parents' effort to head off the ill effects of eating candy on an empty stomach.

When the gifts under the tree were opened, the left-over wrapping paper was as much a part of Christmas festivities as the icicle-draped tree. Then there were our Christmas stockings, each of which offered up not only such practical things as toothpaste and a new toothbrush, but also an orange and nuts.

The afternoon was taken in visiting friends' homes to see what they got. If there was enough time, and if we could get a key to the high school gym, the boys would go off and play basketball.

As the years go by, many of these traditions live on with our family, with some additions picked up along the way. One of our sweetest Christmas traditions began years ago when my wife, Sharon, baked bread or some other treat, and we visited the widows who have become special to our family. Over the years that list has grown, and those visits are so much a part of the season that during a recent Christmas, although we were living out of the country, two of our daughters, Hillary and Mary, made the visits on their own initiative before joining us for the holidays. A bond has developed between us, and we share special experiences with each one as we visit around

Christmastime. From these wonderful women our family receives far more than we give.

It will be a long time before we forget the Christmas we spent in the Philippines. Four of our five children were able to join us for the holidays. The only ones missing were our daughter Kim, her husband, Robert, and our granddaughter, Hillary Jane, who were living in Omaha. Kim was expecting our second grandchild any day.

Christmas in the Philippines is a festive occasion. Filipinos working all over the world are greeted with "Maligayang Pagbabalik" as they return home for Christmas. The Philippines has not lost the sacred side of Christmas, and the celebration is filled with the Christ child as well as other festivities.

There is no Thanksgiving to mark the approach to Christmas, so decorations appear early. The snow is missing, but everything else is there, and the spirit of Christmas in the people and the decorations cannot be missed.

On Christmas Eve day we made our way as a family to a nearby orphanage that was run by an order of Catholic nuns. We brought with us homemade cookies, but mostly we wanted to spend time with the children. Children are usually brought there by a single parent and can stay for up to six months while the parent—usually the mother—looks for work and tries to get her life in order. The mothers visit from time to time, but some children are abandoned and are put up for adoption.

No country is more family oriented than the Philippines. Family and extended family are the heart of Philippine life, so the mothers who bring their children to the orphanage are in the most difficult circumstances.

Most of the children do not understand any of this, and they are torn by seeing the only person they love come and go. For some children there are no visits at all.

We arrived in the afternoon as nap time was ending. The children's beds were in three large rooms—one for the babies, one for boys up to age six, and one for girls up to age six. Each child had a bed that was much like a crib, although larger. It would be impossible to keep the mattresses clean, so the beds had a tightly woven, weblike fabric stretched onto their frames. The beds were metal and it appeared they were washed down from time to time because the floor was damp immediately underneath—a practical way to guard against the spread of diseases brought in by the children.

I must confess that, as we went into the babies' room, I looked around for a baby who did not look too ill. My sons and daughters, however, three of whom had served missions, went immediately to the children who looked the worst and picked them up and held them. These children were the ones who probably received the least attention normally. We were all gradually caught up in the innocence of little babies and the similarity to the Christ child and the manger. Here were children who needed us.

The little boys up to age six were in the second room. They were still in their beds when we arrived, and although none were asleep, there was not a sound.

Some twenty or thirty sets of beautiful brown eyes were trained on us.

My eldest son went to the first crib and said, "My name's Kevin," and reached down to pick the boy up. In minutes pandemonium broke loose. Children who had just finished their naps poured out onto the floor, and we all had more than we could hold. I had one in my arms, and two were holding onto my legs.

As it came time to go, the child in my arms pointed to places in the room, and we would go there. It soon became apparent that he did not want me to put him down. Each time I tried, he would hold onto me with his legs until I almost had to tear him away. At that moment, I wished I could take him home. In his eyes was the look of abandonment. We would try to come back and visit again.

There was another little boy I will not soon forget. He never got out of his bed and would not let anyone pick him up. His eyes were dull and unfocused with the look of someone who was confused and had given up—such young eyes to be filled with such sorrow. My son Alex took his hat off and put it on the boy's head, but there was no response.

As we headed for the next room, we were joined by the Sister who ran the home. She apologized for not meeting us at the door and explained that she was busy arranging an adoption with an Australian couple. She took an immediate liking to my wife, Sharon, and held her hand and talked as we climbed the steps to the girls' room. There were no religious barriers here—just people doing what they could to alleviate some of the

suffering and misery in the world, the suffering of little children.

In the little girls' room I met Pauline. She was probably six and was a little taller than the other girls. She stood looking out the window and would not look at us. Pauline was waiting for the mother who had brought her there. It was hard to know whether the wait was in vain.

I spoke to her, but she did not answer. I gently pulled her away from the window and picked her up. She held herself stiff, as if she did not want to be held. I walked around the room, talking about everything I could think of, but Pauline did not say a word. Finally I put her down and began to go, but she reached out and grabbed my hand and held on. Pauline and I had had a whole conversation, and she had not said a word.

We were all quiet as we walked down the winding driveway to the car. We had had an experience that transcended everything else we would do for Christmas that year. I thought of the words of a hymn:

> Come, O thou King of Kings!
> We've waited long for thee,
> With healing in thy wings
> To set thy people free.
> (Hymns, no. 59.)

We talked about that experience in the days that followed. It was hard to know the fate of the children we visited. Some might even become street children. But for the grace of God, we may have started life there. We learned anew that the Lord expects us to alleviate suffering and sorrow as best we can, just as he did while he was here. We remembered that the meaning of Christ and Christmas includes heavenly parents who know and care and understand, and a Savior who can heal and who will prevail in a world of pain and suffering. We were reminded that the way of the restored gospel of Jesus Christ includes serving our fellowmen.

This is the meaning of Christmas.

Christmas with Family

ELDER LINO ALVAREZ

When Argelia and I got married, we wanted to share our life with our extended family, our parents and our brothers and sisters, especially during Christmas and New Year's. It was not easy for us, as we were not living in the same city, so we decided to stay with her family in Piedras Negras, Coahuila, for Christmas and with my relatives in Saltillo, Coahuila, for New Year's. Although we were not able to do it every year, we always tried to keep in touch with our family, and were able to teach our children about the importance of sharing this beautiful season with our beloved ones. The experiences we shared together were great opportunities for our children to get to know their grandparents, uncles, aunts, and cousins and to strengthen our family ties.

It was wonderful for our children to be able to hear their grandparents share their testimonies of Jesus Christ as well as the priceless teachings they had gained through their lives. Their beautiful family histories helped us to know them better and to love them more. We loved to watch our children light their sparklers and enjoy with their cousins the delicious Mexican food and treats.

The most important Christmas experiences for us were those when, with our children, Argelia Margarita, Lino Alberto, and Jose David, we talked about Christ's life and his teachings in order to live more closely in accordance with his example. When for any reason we could not visit with grandparents, we stayed together in our own home and tried to find ways to bring happiness to our fellowmen.

One thing we enjoyed was "inviting Christ" to our family home evening the Monday before Christmas. In a family council some time earlier, we would select a family or individual from our ward whom we could invite to our home evening closest to Christmas Day. We always invited those who had been a good influence in our lives, whose Christlike behavior was a good example to follow.

At the start of our home evening, we explained to our guests that it was a special night for us, a night in which we wanted to invite Christ into our home, and that we were in fact inviting them because their lives were symbolic of Christ's life. We told them with humbled hearts that they had been a good example to us of how to live as the Savior lived.

Every time we did so, we felt the Spirit of Christ flooding our home and our hearts. The friendship and love for our guests were strengthened and we made the effort to follow their good example throughout the year.

Another of our favorite family customs was to set our clocks ahead on Christmas Eve. When it was eight o'clock for everybody else, for our family it was twelve o'clock. We would have dinner together at "twelve o'clock" and then go into the living room, where we took turns reading the story of Christ's birth found in chapter 2 of Luke, singing Christmas hymns between verses. Sometimes our children played the parts of Mary, Joseph, the shepherds, baby Jesus, and so on. Afterwards we went to bed, leaving the Christmas presents to be opened next morning.

For the Alvarez family, Christmas and New Year's are always beautiful opportunities to enjoy family togetherness.

The Greatest Gift

ELDER DALLAS N. ARCHIBALD

The cold, brisk morning air of winter instantly turned Ron's breath into a small cloud of vapor and made his skin tingle. He'd left his coat inside when he stepped onto the back porch of his home. For a few minutes he wanted to be by himself and think, and the change from the warmth of the house to the crisp, frosty air outside was invigorating.

Dawn was just beginning to break and he could see, silhouetted by the light on the horizon, the dark shapes of the pine trees along the back fence. His friends and neighbors continually kidded him about his devotion to those trees, and always he explained that these weren't ordinary pine trees. They were Christmas trees, homegrown, and with an eternal purpose.

His only child, Nancy, had been born on the tenth of December, just fifteen days before Christmas. Early the next spring, as soon as the ground thawed, Ron planted a small blue spruce in the far corner of the backyard beside the fence. Before that, though, he had done some research, talking with forestry experts and even making a special trip to a nearby university. It was with this newly obtained knowledge that he selected the blue spruce, which, in accordance with the climatic conditions of his area, would be the right size for a Christmas tree in a little less than eight years. Armed with soil-test kits, proper nutrients, equipment for shaping, and, most important, a theme from the scriptures, he had put in the first tree. And each year afterward for six years another seedling had been planted. In this way, Ron had initiated his own special Christmas tradition.

On Nancy's eighth birthday, Ron took the afternoon off from work and went home early. Bundled up in winter clothes he, his wife, Mary, and Nancy had gone to the backyard. There, as a family, they had cut down the first of the seven trees planted in an evenly spaced row along the fence. They cut the tree just above the bottom few branches because, Ron explained, one of these branches would curl up toward the sun; seven years later, when Nancy turned fifteen, it would be the Christmas tree for that year.

Both Ron and Mary knew that children, like pine trees, need proper soil, proper nutrients, and proper shaping both spiritually and temporally. This was one of those shaping, teaching times—an especially important one, as Nancy was preparing to be baptized. Ron felt a ruffle of excitement inside. He'd waited eight years for this day.

After the tree had been secured in its stand and placed in its holiday location in the living room, Ron began. "Nancy, stand back and tell me what you see."

With a squeal of delight and youthful joy she replied immediately, "A pretty tree, Daddy."

"And what did Father Lehi see first in his dream?"

She thought for a moment this time before answering, "A pretty tree."

"Go and get the Book of Mormon from the bookshelf," he suggested, "and as we decorate the tree let's see what comparisons we can make."

As the family took turns reading from chapter eleven of First Nephi, Ron pointed out that Nephi, through the assistance of the Spirit, had seen the Christmas story in a vision. Nephi wanted to see the same things his father, Lehi, had seen in the dream, and an angel had opened the understanding of heaven to him. After he was shown the tree his father had seen, Nephi expressed a desire to know the interpretation of this vision. In response he was taught of the birth of the Savior. The angel then asked Nephi if he now knew the meaning of the tree in his father's dream, and Nephi answered, "Yea, it is the love of God." Years later another disciple of Jesus Christ, John, would say, "For God so loved the world, that he gave his only begotten Son."

(John 3:16.) The love of God for us is represented in his Son, Jesus Christ, Ron explained.

The rod of iron, which is the word of God as contained in the holy scriptures, and also the words of the living servants of God on this earth, will lead us to the fountain of living waters, or to the tree of life, which represent the love of God. Jeremiah was told that the Lord is the fountain of living waters. (Jeremiah 2:13.) The fountain of living waters, the tree of life, and the love of God are all symbolic of Jesus Christ. Later, when Nephi was instructing his brothers, he told them that the tree of life with its precious fruit "is the greatest of all the gifts of God." (1 Nephi 15:36.)

After this discussion, Mary gave Nancy a set of scriptures and a picture of the prophet to put beneath the tree. In this way they would be reminded that these are the iron rod that leads to the tree of life—the Savior. Ron explained that the green of the tree represented the hope of eternal life, hope that comes from the Savior and his atonement.

As the family strung the multicolored lights through the tree branches, Ron spoke of the light of Christ. Everyone has it to bring them to the truth, he said, but after her baptism Nancy would enjoy an increase of that light. By the laying on of hands she would receive the gift of the Holy Ghost; then, as long as she was worthy, the Spirit would be her constant companion to protect her, to guide her, and to testify to her of Jesus Christ.

As Ron and Mary, with Nancy's help, hung round, red ornaments on the tree, Ron talked about the blood of Christ, which was shed for our sins so that we through our faithfulness could be cleansed and purified and one day return to the presence of God and have eternal life. The red ornaments on their tree were a symbol of the Atonement.

Although there would be angels and stars in other Christmas decorations in their home, the top of their tree would display something different. That last adornment was a beautiful red bow with flowing tails of red ribbon. Through this they would remember that the tree of life—the Savior—and his atonement are the greatest of all gifts.

That first year, the decorated Christmas tree was like an invitation to have the Savior in their home, and in the comfort of its soft colored lights the family spent many special moments discussing Nancy's baptism, which took place the first Saturday in January.

The next day, for the first time as an official member of the Church, Nancy partook of the sacrament in remembrance of the Savior and his sacrifice. Monday night in family home evening, the family dismantled their "tree of life" and put the decorations away until the next December 10.

Through the years thereafter, Ron found great solace in the row of seven pine trees, each in a different stage of growth. In moments of challenge and of joy, he received spiritual encouragement from them. He worked to nurture and shape the trees knowing that each one, year after year, would play an important role in bringing thoughts of the Savior and his atonement into Christmas.

The morning light was brighter now

and the snowy yard glistened. Ron had stayed on the porch longer than planned. Today, later in the afternoon, Nancy would be home from her college classes. The three of them, he and Mary and Nancy, would be together once again. He looked toward the fence. The tallest of the pine trees this year was the last one in the row. Almost twenty-one years had passed since he had planted the first. From that planting he had gained another cutting by redirecting a lower branch. Seven years ago he had torn up that stump and planted a new tree in its place. Now it was time to cut the last of the original seven, and next spring a new seedling would be planted in its spot.

Over the years, Ron and Mary had sought the guidance of the Spirit, praying that their shaping and nurturing would give Nancy the proper direction in her life to bring her to an active knowledge of the Savior in applying his teachings. This evening they would again decorate a tree and review the account of Nephi. And again, as when she was eight, the discussions would be in anticipation of an event that was soon to be. Her mission application papers had been forwarded to Salt Lake City by the stake president and hopefully, before the first Saturday of the new year, she would receive her call from the prophet of the Lord to go and teach others of the tree of life and its precious fruit.

The winter air suddenly made Ron shiver. He turned and opened the door. It was time to go to work, but he would be back home a little early today. It was Nancy's birthday—time to begin Christmas again.

Temple Blessings for Christmas

ELDER YOSHIHIKO KIKUCHI

In the spring of 1990, around April conference time, my wife and I began to have dreams about deceased friends and Saints we had known when we joined the Church many years before. In our dreams we both saw the same people—not just one or two people, but nine, from a small branch in Muroran, Hokkaido, Japan. They had passed away within several years of each other. We saw these people many times in our dreams. We thought we were just getting old.

One day my wife said to me, "I wonder if the temple work for these people has been finished." Because they were members of the Church in good standing who had gone beyond the veil without ever being able to attend the temple, we thought the Church would have automatically done the temple work for them.

My wife's question really stirred my soul. I began to research the records of our friends, to learn the status of their temple work. I found that, except for one sister, none of them had had their temple work finished. I was able to trace their deceased parents and families also.

One of the brothers on our list was a man by the name of Ishii, who was taught by stake missionaries. He was a very famous radio actor at one time, but he got multiple sclerosis while he was still acting. When we baptized him, a few people had to hold his whole body and immerse him in the water. When he came to church meetings, we young priesthood bearers went out to get him with a wagon. Sometimes we carried him on our shoulders. (In those days, none of the Church members in our area owned private cars.) Brother Ishii became a Junior Sunday School teacher, working with my wife, who was Junior Sunday School superintendent before she married. He presented some wonderful picture shows and cartoons for the children. He died a few years later.

Before I left on my mission my girlfriend, who later became my wife, and I had the privilege to visit with another woman many times. My wife tells her story about this woman:

"Before I married, I served as a stake missionary. One day we found a sister named Furukawa. We learned that she had joined the Church before World War

II. She had married outside the Church because it was war time. Eventually she fell away. Then she lost her husband and son during the war.

"After I was released from the stake mission, I continued to visit her frequently for the next few years. Later, when her health declined and she was very weak, I visited her almost every day. One day when I went to see her, her home was empty. The neighbors said she had had a sudden stroke, had lost her memory, and could not understand anything. Consequently, the city welfare people had taken her to a nursing home. I was relieved and happy that she had twenty-four-hour care. I did not visit her for a little while. Then shortly before the Christmas season, I went to the nursing home, where I was told she could not understand anyone and didn't remember anything. I pursued anyway, and as I opened the door of her room she rushed into my bosom, calling me by name and giving me a hug. We cried together. She had remembered my name even after her massive stroke. Shortly after that, she passed away quietly."

Brother Ishii, Sister Furukawa, and others came to our dreams many times, which prompted us to begin serious research. We found their records, and also those of their parents. My wife and I had the privilege of doing the temple work for each one of them, including sealing them to their parents. While I was in the ordinance room with a kind ordinance worker, I felt Brother Ishii's love. In my mind I said to him in Japanese, "Brother Ishii, you have been waiting for a long time. Congratulations! Now soon you can be sealed to your wife." I felt his gentle love and kind spirit, as though he were saying to me, "Thank you." It was a time of great rejoicing.

Finally, in 1993 during the Thanksgiving and Christmas season, we finished all the temple ordinances for the people we had dreamed about. It was a memorable Christmastime activity. All the friends we knew when we joined the Church, those who have now gone beyond the veil, have received the saving ordinances. They came all the way to the United States to let us know that they really needed those ordinances in order to receive the full blessing of the Savior's atonement. They knew they must receive these ordinances to ensure that their lives will be exalted in the eternities to come.

This was a very special Christmas, because I felt "the love of God" (1 Nephi 11:22–23), "the condescension of God" (1 Nephi 11:16), the birth of the Savior. I felt that the blessings of the Savior's sacred birth were embraced by our friends. I'm sure it was also a very special Christmas in the spirit world, and that these people rejoiced as did my wife and I.

Christmas Thoughts of Home and of Prague

ELDER RUSSELL M. NELSON

At the Nelson home we enjoy many Christmas traditions. A small circular photograph of each member of the family is rimmed with ribbon and hung as an ornament to decorate our tree. Children and grandchildren love to identify their own pictures among the many. We have been doing this for so many years that the pictures now are no longer current, thus adding interest and making identification a little more challenging. And oh, how the children love their grandmother's (Sister Nelson's) assortment of small dolls collected from various countries throughout the world! Those dolls are also nestled among the branches of the decorated tree. Grandmother's cookies, cakes, candies, and candlelight dinners are greatly cherished and long remembered by all. Christmas gifts, gatherings, and gladness are important components of our traditions at this, our favorite time of the year.

Blessed with ten children, our home has always been one where togetherness is the normal way of life. In years past, Christmas Eve served to accentuate that spirit as all of the children wanted to sleep in the same room on that special night. Even the first two or three sons-in-law were naturally expected to submit to that tradition—until they finally persuaded their partners that such a custom required revision.

One tradition that hasn't been revised is greeting Christmas morning with music. When our children were younger, they would surround their parents' bed and sing songs of love for their mother and father and of their adoration for the Christ child. That tradition we still enjoy, although we don't see our nine daughters and one son encircling our bed. All but the youngest are established in homes of their own. But we enjoy any and every member of the family who may have chosen to spend the night at our home, including sons-in-law and grandchildren. Those serenades still seem mighty sweet to us.

Music has always been an important part of our family activities, especially at Christmastime. One night preceding each Christmas, our extended family—brothers, sisters, uncles, aunts, cousins (and our parents before they passed away)—crowd into our living room for the children to stage their annual Christmas pageant. We read the scriptural accounts of the Lord's birth from the second chapter of Luke and from the Book of Mormon. Then we sing carols, accompanied by pianists and other instrumentalists. Of course, we sing the whimsical ditties about Santa, Rudolph the red-nosed reindeer, the partridge in a pear tree, and many more. We get warmed up on those numbers. Then we sing our favorites about the Savior, including "Away in a Manger," "The First Noel," "I Heard the Bells on Christmas Day," "Hark! the Herald Angels Sing," "With Wondering Awe," "O Little Town of Bethlehem," "It Came upon the Midnight Clear," "Joy to the World," and "Oh, Come, All Ye Faithful." By the time we sing our closing song, "Silent Night," we truly feel the real spirit of Christmas.

Just as the Savior's mother pondered sacred things in her heart, so some of our deepest feelings of reverence and gratitude are unspoken and unsung. Some are felt only deeply within. They are so sacred that speaking openly of them would seem in some way to desecrate them. I'm sure we all feel that way when we sing and ponder the birth, the mission, and the atonement of the Lord Jesus Christ.

At Christmastime, when our family sings "Good King Wenceslas," I find myself silently reflecting on the real meaning of words in that song. They are seldom understood, and their connection with Christmas seems obscure.

Good King Wenceslas looked out
On the Feast of Stephen,
When the snow lay round about,
Deep, and crisp, and even:
Brightly shone the moon that night,
Though the frost was cruel,
When a poor man came in sight,
Gath'ring winter fuel.

Several other verses follow, ending with the lines,

Therefore, Christian men, be sure,
Wealth or rank possessing,
Ye who now will bless the poor,
Shall yourselves find blessing.

In spite of that nice Christian reminder to give to the poor, the song has never been one of our favorites, and still isn't, really. But my call as an Apostle and my many visits to the country of Czechoslovakia have given me a greater appreciation for it.

What was the "Feast of Stephen"? Who was "Good King Wenceslas"?

The Feast of Stephen relates to the Stephen who was stoned to death in Jerusalem. I presume that Stephen was one of the first Christian martyrs after the crucifixion of the Lord. Over the years, the martyrdom of Stephen and the feast that commemorated the event became associated with the birth of the Christ. So these two dates were interlocked—the birth of Christ, celebrated December 25, and the Feast of Stephen, observed December 26.

King Wenceslas, more correctly spelled *Wenceslaus*, was born in the year 907 near Prague. *Wenceslaus* is the English translation of his real name, which in the Czech language is Svátý Václav. He was one of the first Christian martyrs. In Czechoslovakia he strove to bring peace between the Christians and the non-Christians. For his Christian belief and commitment, he went to a martyr's death on the doorsteps of a church in Prague. Thereafter he became the patron saint of all Czechoslovakia.

Perhaps the best known square in downtown Prague bears the name of Wenceslaus (in English), or Václav (in Czech). Even through more than forty years of political oppression, the statue of good King Wenceslaus has stood on the square as a silent symbol of the enduring spirit of Christianity.

The first time Sister Nelson and I went to Wenceslaus Square in downtown Prague, it was starkly deserted and quiet during the dark stillness of night. There was a telephone booth at one end of the square. While we were standing at the opposite end, we could hear the voice of an individual in the telephone booth because there was no one else stirring in Wenceslaus Square. In subsequent years, our visits to the Square and downtown Prague again found very few people outside at night.

Following the "velvet revolution" in 1989 and the crumbling of communism in Czechoslovakia, the mood in Prague changed. The last time we were in Wenceslaus Square (1991), the place was teeming with people, talking, singing, and enjoying their newfound freedom.

It was in Wenceslaus Square that the "velvet revolution" occurred. Thousands and thousands of people filled the Square that November in 1989, demanding the overthrow of their restrictive regime. A month later, on December 29, 1989, a man became the president of this new democracy who just a few weeks before had been imprisoned for his anti-establishment beliefs and for his advocacy of freedom and religious opportunity. Significantly, the man elected as the first president of the new democracy—who also became the first president of the Czech Republic—is named Václav Havel.

When my thoughts turn to Prague, I ponder the faith of Church leaders of yesteryear when the Church was first recognized in Czechoslovakia. Missionaries labored with dignity, until war and its spoils cancelled those privileges. I also remember those leaders with whom I labored in seeking recognition for the Church in Czechoslovakia. Elder Hans B. Ringger of the Seventy, and our district president in Prague, Jiři Šnederfler, and his dear wife, Olga, were valiant companions and pioneers. During the early days of our inquiries, Elder Ringger and I learned that recognition could be formally requested only by a Czechoslovakian member of the Church. So we went to the home of the Šnederflers with that very disturbing information. Brother and Sister Šnederfler understood the risks, because Czechs had not fared well if their religious affiliation had become known. Humbly, Brother Šnederfler said, "I will go." He and Olga were willing to be martyrs if need be, as were King Wenceslaus, the Prophet Joseph Smith, and others.

On February 21, 1990, The Church of Jesus Christ of Latter-day Saints again received official recognition and became registered in Czechoslovakia after many years of restricted existence. Now we have a mission there with congregations of committed converts and stalwart Saints. Later, Jiři Šnederfler and his dear Olga were called to serve as president and matron of the Freiberg Germany Temple.

These and related thoughts flood my mind as the strains of "Good King Wenceslas" are sung at Christmastime. I think of Christian martyrs, of pioneers, of freedom, and of all who have gone before to make life for us as sweet and meaningful as it is. Because of their pain and tears, my cup of joy is full at Christmastime.

For such marvelous memories and all good gifts, Sister Nelson and I express our deepest gratitude. We love the Lord and his Church and acknowledge his beneficent hand in all that are near and dear to us. At Christmas and throughout the year we appreciate all the Savior's gifts—especially the blessing of being members of his Church. He is, in very deed, the Good King who bestows the riches of eternity upon those who love him.

A Far Greater Gift

ELDER JAMES M. PARAMORE

A number of years ago our family had the privilege of serving a mission in Belgium and France. We had six small children, including a new baby born in that country. Before Christmas we had written home for some clothing and Christmas gifts for our children. They did not arrive in time for Christmas as we had hoped.

As we sat together Christmas Eve reading the New Testament and the account of the birth of the Savior, there was a little melancholy because there would not be many gifts. But as we read the words about the gift our Father in Heaven had given, his beloved Son, Jesus, we realized that there were many in our city who needed help. So we quickly gathered together some of our possessions and a Christmas box of groceries and sought out one of those families.

As we all visited that tiny apartment and began to sing Christmas carols, our hearts were full as perhaps never before. We felt the spirit of giving, we felt the spirit of those who were receiving, and we felt the spirit of our Father in Heaven.

We returned to our home that Christmas Eve with a far greater gift than those gifts we had anticipated from home. Truly, the only real gift is the gift of oneself.

This chapter is adapted from "A Far Greater Gift," © The Church of Jesus Christ of Latter-day Saints. Used by permission.

A Hong Kong Christmas

ELDER KWOK YUEN TAI

Christmas season in Hong Kong, just as in many other large cities, has turned into a major annual commercial opportunity. The colorful lights decorating arcades, streets, and high-rises around the Victoria Harbor enhance the festive mood of the city. The attractive displays in shop windows could be very tempting. All of these are just very commercial!

The three years I spent as mission president of the Hong Kong Mission have, however, given me a different perception of the Christmas season. It was quite an adjustment during the first year without the family around. But mission activities and experiences brought the true spirit of Christmas, unforgettable joy that I had never felt before.

Our missionaries sang in busy shopping arcades, proclaiming the birth of the Savior and his mission on earth. Watching their impressive performance, I felt a great sense of pride and satisfaction. It was a special privilege to work with these wonderful young people. Reflected on the faces of the onlookers were expressions of celebration, admiration, and sometimes dismay. Many of them were so impressed that they wanted to know more about these young missionaries and their message.

The "Santa Hats" project organized by my sweet companion, Hui Hua, brought lots of fun and blessings to our missionaries. All the hard work of making dozens of hats paid off when we saw our missionaries happily using them in their street activities. With Santa hats on, the carol-singing missionaries attracted many passing people, who stopped to watch. Some even visited with our missionaries. We sang with one group outside the Kowloon Tong Mass Transit Railway Station, greeting the passersby, including a unit of patrolling police officers. We received in return smiles, applause, and, most of all, opportunities to introduce the Church and the gospel. I even got a referral on the spot!

The mission home kitchen was busy making cookies for our "Christmas Cookies" project. Cookies filled the kitchen and the family room. The smell was always a delight! Over three thousand cookies were baked and packed with Christmas wrappings. Missionaries enjoyed presenting them, together with a story of the first Christmas, to local leaders, needy Church members, and parents of local missionaries. Many of the parents were not Church members. Their hearts were softened when they received our missionaries and heard firsthand reports about the work of their missionary sons and daughters. One mother and three sisters accepted the gospel and were baptized by their own missionary son. Through this project, we were able to reach out to many people and share with them the true spirit of Christmas.

The Lord has specially blessed our missionaries in their activities. Despite the busy schedule, December has always been a month of many conversions. On one Christmas Eve, fourteen people were baptized in just one district of our mission. The excitement over the baptisms was just like that of having a white Christmas!

Early on Christmas morning 1991, we joined the members and missionaries of the Shaukiwan Ward to visit the Cape Collinson Correctional Center. The Center was on a steep mountain slope overlooking a quiet bay. Some 230 young men under eighteen years of age assembled in a hall. All were repeat offenders of serious criminal acts. Among them were many handsome, innocent faces,

and some looked perturbed. If they could just have had the gospel early in their lives, what might they have become!

They enjoyed the games we brought along, and the carol singing. We showed the Church video "The Prodigal Son," capturing the attention of most of them. Many eyes were wet.

We left the group to visit a few youths in solitary confinement. We stood in front of each cell, singing carols and delivering our Christmas and New Year greetings. Obviously touched by our visit, many became emotional. It was a very special Christmas Day for all of us.

On Boxing Day (December 26) three hundred investigators, local missionary parents, and missionaries assembled for a special fireside in the Kowloon Tong Chapel. Missionaries told stories, sang carols, and shared the meaning of the commonly seen Christmas symbols. All who attended had a good time and returned to their homes with a better understanding of the true meaning of Christmas.

These indeed were some glorious Christmas experiences in the mission field in Hong Kong. Peace will prevail on earth and goodwill can be among mankind if we always have the true spirit of Christmas in our hearts.

Christmas Experiences

ELDER EARL C. TINGEY

I grew up in the little community of Centerville, Utah, ten miles north of Salt Lake City. It was a small, friendly Mormon community consisting of two wards. Everyone knew everyone. I was the oldest of ten children and we had many relatives in the community. Celebrating in Centerville was my idea of a "traditional Christmas."

Several days before Christmas day, my parents would organize food baskets containing fruits and vegetables from our storehouse. We children were instructed to take the baskets to selected widows and less fortunate families in our ward. We were told to do it in such a way that the families would not know from whom the food came. I have since determined that most of the families suspected that it was from my parents.

On Christmas Eve, the entire ward gathered at the recreation hall for a nativity pageant. The program concluded with the appearance of Santa Claus. Commercial Santas did not commonly appear before Christmas Eve in our town.

In Centerville, the weather was cold at Christmastime. There was generally snow on the ground in town, and much more in the nearby mountains. Winter sports activities dominated the Christmas season. Sleigh riding was our most popular winter activity. First South, from the top of the hill to the bottom at Main Street, was designated by the mayor and the chief of police as a sleigh-riding hill; all cars would stop and then carefully cross the street to avoid the sledding children. We also loved ice skating on the pasture ponds west of the city. It never seriously occurred to me that anyone could enjoy a "real" Christmas in anything other than a winter atmosphere.

All of this changed when I departed for my mission to Australia in November 1954. I traveled across the Pacific Ocean on a small freighter, stopping at many Pacific islands on the way. On Christmas Day, our little ship anchored in the harbor at Auckland, New Zealand.

Because the ship was not scheduled to depart for Australia until after New Year's Day, we missionaries were on our own. We went ashore and booked ourselves into the nearby Waverly Hotel.

(The room charge was $6.00 per night.) This was the first night in my life that I stayed in a hotel. I felt very alone and far removed from the Christmas spirit I had felt all my life.

As I lay on the bed in the hotel room, attempting to sleep, I visualized the wintry Christmas my family was having. Outside my hotel room it was midsummer. It felt more like the Fourth of July than Christmas. How could anyone celebrate Christmas in such an environment? That was when I first realized that half of the people in the world celebrate Christmas in a warm climate.

Since that first Christmas Day in Auckland, New Zealand, I have enjoyed eight additional Christmases in the southern hemisphere. Two more occurred when I was a young, single missionary. Twenty years later I celebrated three Christmases in Sydney, Australia, with my family while serving there as the mission president. More recently, my wife and I have enjoyed the past three Christmases in Johannesburg, South Africa, where I served as a member of the Africa Area Presidency.

In all of these nine Christmas experiences, I have learned that celebrating and honoring Christmas depends not so much on where you are, but on how you feel about the Savior and your fellowmen. I have also discovered that during the Christmas season people develop tender and loving feelings toward their friends and associates. Something about the spirit of Christmas causes men to show love and warmth toward all others. Hatred and indifference seem to dissipate during the Christmas season.

One of my favorite Christmas stories depicts the genuine feelings of brotherhood that can develop during this blessed season. It is a true story that took place in France in the early months of World War I.

Trench warfare was the way of that war, and in this particular section of French countryside, the British were dug in only a few hundred yards away from the Germans. On Christmas Eve, drifting across from the German side, was heard a familiar-sounding carol, "Stille Nacht, heilige Nacht." A British soldier joined in with the English words, "Silent night, holy night."

Soon others blended their voices with the pair, and carols flew back and forth through the night. As dawn lit the sky on Christmas Day, the troops crept cautiously out and began to meet each other, exchanging small gifts of candy and cigarettes, playing an impromptu soccer game. Signs appeared on both sides, in two languages: "Merry Christmas."

But by midmorning the officers had caught wind of the situation and ordered the soldiers back into their trenches to fire at each other once more.

"And the soldiers obeyed. The war, as history tragically records, destroyed almost that entire generation of young men on both sides. But there was an indelible memory in the minds of those who lived to recall that first Christmas at the front . . . the memory of a few hours when their master had been neither King nor Kaiser, but the Prince of Peace." (*Guidepost Magazine*, December 1989.)

Room in the Inn

ELDER NEIL L. ANDERSEN

On a bright, crisp winter afternoon we pointed our Volkswagen van toward the mission home in Bordeaux, France. It was December 24, 1990, and we were on our way home for Christmas.

My wife, Kathy, and I, along with our four children—Camey, age fourteen, Brandt, thirteen, Kristen, ten, and Derek, eight—had just experienced a week to remember. Because of the distances involved in our mission, we had not brought the missionaries together for a Christmas celebration. Rather, we had traveled as a family to every city in the mission, bringing a feeling of family togetherness, involving the children in sharing a special Christmas program. Our family had rejoiced with each of the missionaries in the great privilege of sharing the restored gospel of Christ at this glorious time of year.

On our final day we had been joined by four wonderful missionaries. The large blue van, now full, was filled as well with the Christmas spirit, and Christmas carols and favorite stories made the travel time pass quickly. Kristen and Derek were becoming more excited with each hour as they anticipated the surprises Christmas morning would bring. We could almost smell the turkey dinner being prepared at the mission home by a wonderful missionary couple awaiting our return. The feeling of Christmas was in the air.

It was not until late in the afternoon that we realized there might be a problem. For much of the morning we had experienced some difficulty in shifting from one gear to another. We had stopped to check the level of the transmission fluid, but all seemed to be in order. Now, with darkness setting in and our van still two hours from Bordeaux, third, fourth, and fifth gears stopped functioning altogether.

We limped along the tree-lined country road in second gear. It would be impossible to drive to Bordeaux in this condition, and we looked for possible help. Our first hope was a convenience store just preparing to close. I asked about possible rental-car locations or train stations nearby. We were far from any city of any size, however, and my questions brought only an insensitive chuckle from the employee hurrying to close the store. No help was offered and no encouragement was given.

I returned to the van. The concern and disappointment showed on the faces of our younger children. Would they not be home for Christmas Eve? Would they spend this most special night of the year in a crowded mission van? After bringing happiness and cheer to missionaries far from home, would their Christmas come alongside a forgotten French country road far from their own home?

Kristen, age ten, knew to whom we could appeal, and immediately suggested a prayer. Many times as a family we had prayed for those in need—for the missionaries, the investigators, the Church members, our leaders, the French people, our own family. We bowed in prayer and humbly asked for help.

By now it was dark. The van crept forward, moving at a jogger's pace through the pine forest. We were hoping to reach a little town just three miles ahead. Soon our lights caught the small sign with the arrow directing us to Villeneuve-de-Marsan.

Although we had driven the two-lane road from Pau to Bordeaux many times, never had we journeyed off the highway the 1.5 kilometers to the little town of Villeneuve-de-Marsan. As we hobbled into the town, the scene was like many small French villages. Homes and small shops were attached one to another, crowding the narrow road leading into town. People had closed their window shutters early and the streets were dark and deserted. The lights in the ancient Catholic church in the center of town showed the one sign of life, as they glowed in preparation for the traditional midnight mass. We rolled past the church, and the van hesitated and then stopped completely. Fortunately, we found ourselves in front of a lovely country inn. The lights were on, and we determined that this was our last chance for help.

To avoid overwhelming those in the inn, Kathy, Camey, and the missionaries stayed in the van while I took the three younger children inside. I explained our situation to the young woman at the front desk. She could see the beleaguered faces of my children, and kindly asked us to wait while she called the innkeeper, Mr. Francis Darroze.

As we waited for Mr. Darroze to arrive I silently said a prayer of thanksgiving. We might not make it back to Bordeaux for the night, but how good of our Father in Heaven to lead us to a clean hotel! I shuddered as I realized how easily we could have spent the night in the van in a remote area of France. I could see a restaurant in the next room, and was amazed to see it open on Christmas Eve. We would have a good meal, a hot shower, and a comfortable sleep.

Mr. Darroze arrived in the clothing of a traditional French chef, with his double-breasted chef's coat buttoned all the way up to his chin. He was the owner of the hotel, a man of importance in the community. His warm eyes and quick smile communicated that he was a gentleman as well.

I told him of our dilemma, of the ten of us in the van, and of our destination in Bordeaux. As he noticed my accent, I added that we were Americans and in one sentence told him why we were in France.

He instantly sought to help us. About ten miles away was a medium-sized city with an active train schedule. He called to ask about the next train to Bordeaux, but found that it would not leave until 10:15 Christmas morning. All rental-car companies in that larger city were closed.

The disappointment was most certainly evident in the faces of my young children. I asked Mr. Darroze if he would have room in the inn for our family and the four missionaries to spend the night. Although we wouldn't make it home, at least it was a great blessing to have found such suitable accommodations.

Mr. Darroze looked at the children. He had known us only a few minutes, but his heart was touched with the brotherhood that crosses all oceans and makes us one family. The spirit of Christmas giving filled his soul. "Mr. Andersen," he said, "of course I have rooms here that you can rent. But you do not want to spend Christmas Eve here in the inn. Children should be home as they await the excitement of Christmas morning. I will lend you my car, and you can go to Bordeaux tonight."

I was amazed at his thoughtfulness. Most people would view strangers, and especially foreigners like us, with caution. I thanked him, but explained that there were ten of us and a small French car would never be sufficient.

He hesitated momentarily, but his hesitation was not to diminish the gift but to expand it. "At my farm about ten miles from here I have an old van. It is used for farming and has only the two seats in front. It will travel only at about 45 miles per hour and I am not certain the heater works well. But if you want it, I will drive you the ten miles to my farm to get it."

The children jumped for joy. I reached into my pocket for cash or my credit cards. He quickly shook his head and his finger in disapproval. "No," he said, "I will take nothing. You can bring my van back to me when you get time after Christmas. It is Christmas Eve. Take your family home."

Sometime shortly after midnight the lights of Bordeaux came into view. The children and the missionaries had fallen asleep in the back of the innkeeper's van. As we drove the familiar streets leading to our home, Kathy and I thanked our kind Heavenly Father for our own Christmas miracle. In a time when only he could bring us home, he heard our prayers. We were home on Christmas Eve, even though in Villeneuve-de-Marsan there was room in the inn.

Giving, Sharing, and Remembering

ELDER CARLOS E. ASAY

Each yuletide season brings to my mind a flood of memorable experiences. However, three of those experiences stand out like lampposts in the chambers of my memory. One involved giving and a young woman by the name of Emily, another centered on sharing and a family bicycle, and a third focused upon remembering and an old Armenian tradition called "the burning of the calendar."

Emily and Giving

Emily, a fifteen-year-old daughter of a stake president, sat across the breakfast table from me. It was a few weeks before Christmas and the home was adorned with a Christmas tree and other traditional decorations. Some of the lively mealtime conversation with family members was about school, the stake conference, the delicious food being served, Santa Claus, and anticipated gifts. As the meal ended, Emily asked, "Elder Asay, if Christ were here with us today, what would you give him?"

I was caught off guard, surprised by the thought-provoking nature of the question. One does not often receive from a teenager an inquiry so timely and of such significance. When I had collected my senses, I responded with these lines from the poet Christina Rossetti:

> *What can I give him, poor as I am?*
> *If I were a shepherd, I would bring a lamb.*
> *If I were a Wise Man, I would do my part.*
> *Yet, what can I give Him? Give my heart.*

I shall never approach another Christmas season without thinking of Emily and her question. Christmas is about Christ and giving. He gave us the precious gifts of immortality and the prospects of eternal life. Surely we owe our hearts and more to him in return for his infinite goodness.

A Family Bicycle and Sharing

My mother and father were not wealthy people. They possessed many things that money cannot buy, but, as to the things of the world, their possessions were precious few. Therefore, Christmas was a challenging time. The issue for them was always, "What can we afford to give our six children this year?"

On one particular Christmas morning we six children, on signal from our parents, bounded out of bed and raced into the living room to see what Santa Claus had brought us. All of the stockings were full of nuts, fruits, and candy. And we observed a few personal items like gloves and handkerchiefs. But there were no large toys or balls or skates of the usual variety. In the center of the room, however, stood a new red bicycle with a card attached. The card read: "To all the children."

It was not an easy thing for six active youngsters—four boys and two girls—to schedule the use of a single bicycle. But we did, and we learned to share! Christmas is for sharing, especially when the shared gift is received from loving parents who give freely of their meager resources.

The Burning of the Calendar and Remembering

Years ago, I was introduced to a wonderful Armenian tradition called "the burning of the calendar." I was serving as a full-time missionary in the old Palestine-Syrian Mission with headquarters in Beirut, Lebanon. The setting was the palatial home of a wealthy merchant in Alexandria, Egypt, where approximately one hundred people had gathered to end the year and to begin another.

The party began early as the host family and guests enjoyed a sumptuous dinner consisting of exotic foods and a wide variety of drinks, including milk for me. People ate and talked and listened to entertainers for several hours. No one, however, became boisterous or unruly during the evening; all showed tremendous respect for the gracious merchant and his home.

As midnight approached, the dining ceased and the mood of the group changed noticeably. I wondered what was going to happen. Quietly, even reverently, the host and his family led the group into a nearby drawing room. No verbal commands were given. Everyone moved as if drawn by a strong, unseen power. I tagged along behind the others, not understanding what was taking place.

Once inside the drawing room, I raised on tiptoe to see over the crowd. I saw our host's mother, the family matriarch, seated in a soft chair surrounded by her children, grandchildren, and invited guests. She was a beautiful old woman with snow-white hair and an angelic countenance. No one spoke; I hardly breathed. I have rarely been in a place or among people outside of the temple where the atmosphere was more solemn or sacred.

Then, just before the stroke of twelve, the butler entered with a large silver tray in his hands. On the tray was a colorful Armenian calendar of the year that was coming to a close. The old woman slowly struck a match and lighted the paper. In perfect silence, we all watched as the burning calendar symbolized the end of the year.

I expected bedlam to break out and the usual New Year's shouts to fill the room. But there were no shouts or wild demonstrations. Another servant entered from the other side of the room. He carried another tray with another colorful calendar on full display. The old woman took from the tray the calendar of the new year and showed it to the group at the stroke of midnight. The timing was perfect.

I thought to myself, now comes the explosion! It didn't. I saw the old woman whisper something to her son, who stood nearby. He in turn whispered to another, and the word passed in this fashion until the wave of whispers reached me. "The lady," said my companion, "knows that you are a minister of the Lord Jesus Christ, and she wonders if you would be willing to lead the group in a New Year's prayer." Though somewhat stunned by the invitation, I said that I would be honored to give the prayer, providing I could give it in my own language. (I feared that my command of the Armenian language was too limited for me to do the occasion justice.)

My response was conveyed by the wave of whispers back to the old woman. To my further surprise, another message was sent to me. My companion explained: "The old lady said that you should pray in your native language. She said that God understands all languages and that we will know what comes from your heart. She also said that you should thank God for the blessings received this past year and ask for his continued blessings in the year ahead."

I prayed in behalf of the group and felt the presence of the Holy Spirit.

Time will never erase the memory of that sacred occasion with friends who remembered God first and last—at the beginning of a new year and the close of the old.

Yes, the yuletide season is a time of giving, sharing, and remembering. God bless us to treasure all the priceless gifts related to the righteous traditions of our lives.

Portions of this chapter have been excerpted from Carlos E. Asay, *Family Pecan Trees* (Salt Lake City: Deseret Book Co., 1992).

Christmas in the Mission Home

ELDER LEGRAND R. CURTIS

Christmastime in a mission home is always a memorable experience. The young missionaries, although glad to be serving the Lord, also have sweet remembrances of home and the family traditions that will be happening there. Our office staff members in Tallahassee, Florida, were dedicated young people determined to serve honorable missions. On Christmas Eve we invited them to the mission home for dinner and the traditional Curtis family program. For many years our family had put together a presentation based on the account of Christ's birth as found in the book of Luke. It was always a very significant Christmas tradition in our home.

We gathered all the bathrobes and articles of clothing necessary to dress the wise men, Joseph and Mary, and other participants, and we found a doll suitable to represent the baby Jesus.

As all present sensed their part in the sacred drama, a sweet spirit filled the home. The missionaries covered their name tags with robes, blankets, and appropriate articles of clothing to assume the roles assigned them.

We held a short rehearsal to acquaint each person with his or her role in our Christmas play. As we sang "Silent Night," "It Came upon the Midnight Clear," "Far, Far Away on Judea's Plains," "Away in a Manger," "Oh, Come, All Ye Faithful," and "The First Noel," our hearts mellowed and our eyes filled with tears.

As I read Luke, chapter 2, verses 1-20, I felt a sweet spirit and love for the Savior.

"And it came to pass in those days, that there went out a decree . . .

"And all went to be taxed, every one into his own city . . .

"And [Mary] brought forth her first-born son, and wrapped him in swaddling clothes . . .

"And there were in the same country shepherds abiding in the field . . .

"And, lo, the angel of the Lord came upon them, and . . . said unto them, . . .

"Unto you is born this day in the city of David a Saviour, which is Christ the Lord.

"And this shall be a sign unto you; Ye

shall find the babe wrapped in swaddling clothes, lying in a manger. . . .

"Glory to God in the highest, and on earth peace, good will toward men. . . .

"And they came with haste, and found Mary, and Joseph, and the babe."

Our missionaries performed as the scriptures indicated, with a reverence and love befitting the sacredness of the story.

The scriptures, the spirit of the young missionaries, and the divine message left a lasting impression on everyone present in the mission home that evening. We truly had felt the message of Christmas—that *Jesus is the Christ*.

Merry Christmas, Murphy

ELDER STEPHEN D. NADAULD

Dear Murphy,

Precious little baby, brand new to this world, welcome to our hearts and to the most glorious of seasons, Christmastime! There is no more blessed or happy time in our family than this, and all hearts and souls come home for Christmas, so you arrived just in time!

We are the parents of your father. We love him and your beautiful mother very much. You won't understand all of what we have to say now, but we're writing anyway to welcome you to our family. You have a wonderful mother and father. Your daddy, our little boy, was born on a warm summer morning in New York. It was Father's Day, 1969. He and your mother grew up as happy children and got married after their missions. Now here you are, born on a cold winter day in Utah, just before Christmas. How thrilled we all are to welcome you to our family! You have come at a wonderful time of year and we want to tell you about what you have to look forward to in the next few weeks when it will be Christmas.

You will come to Manti with us and your beaming new parents to be surrounded by eager extended family: young uncles, curious cousins, grateful grandparents, and lots of loving relatives. The fun will begin even before we reach the little valley town nestled beneath the protection of a temple. From miles away everyone joins in the contest to be the first one to see the temple and shout out the discovery joyfully. Soon enough, there it will be, standing on the white, snow-covered hill, surrounded by pines whose boughs hang heavy with winter's moisture. The whiteness of this holy house is accented by the clearness of the blue sky. The temple is God's house; six generations before you were sealed there eternally.

Practically in the shadow of the temple is Grandpa and Grandma Dyreng's house. It's always big enough for everyone, no matter how many come. There, hearts and hearth have room at Christmastime.

When we drive up the driveway the first thing you'll see is the skating rink Grandpa made on the north side of the barn. He built up berms of grass on the sides, and every winter he floods the lower ground inside the berms with water. Then each night he goes outside in the freezing cold and waters the rink. This way he builds up layers of ice perfect for skating.

Cousins of all sizes will be skating and playing hockey with the puck Grandpa played with as a boy in the 1920s. He has saved it all these years and no one has ever lost it (for long). The little ones will be wobbly on their skates, and there will be some who skate on the insides of their ankles. But little or big, everybody plays together, stocking caps flying out behind, and the fun goes on. Soon someone will have to stop to go with Grandpa down to the workbench to repair a broken hockey stick. It's part of the fun.

Uh-oh, watch out! There goes a child sliding off the roof of the barn and landing on the big bank of snow that has been piled deep for protection. Now we see cousins scrambling, boosting each other up on the roof for yet another ride.

Before we are out of the car, the back door to the house bursts open and there are Grandpa and Grandma to love us home. Grandma will wipe flour off her hands onto her apron before the hug. "We're so glad you made it. Bless you for coming!" they will say, and, Murphy, they will oooh and aaah over you and exclaim what a beautiful, healthy baby you are. We will follow them inside, where Grandma will hurry to her magic corner counter in the kitchen to finish making delicious treats out of dough. Grandpa will put another log on each of the fires burning in the parlor and the

game room, and then he'll be off to tend the caramel ice cream he's freezing for dessert. The warm aromas that greet us from the oven and stove are as real as the hugs and kisses we've just had.

In the dining room, the table is set with beautiful formality. (Grandma believes in using her "finest" for the family.) The china, crystal, and silver sparkle on the starched linen next to the holiday centerpiece. Soon everyone arrives and we find our places for Christmas dinner. This year four more children "graduate" up to the big table, taking the places of the missionaries who have gone to Germany, Peru, Russia, and Uruguay to serve the Lord. The children's table is all giggles and squirms, but becomes quiet when Grandpa, the patriarch, bows his head to talk with Heavenly Father on our behalf and give thanks. Some of us will brush away a tear as we say amen.

Then the eating begins. First there is icy fruit cocktail. (Grandma froze it in jars last fall from fresh cantaloupe, pears, peaches, raspberries, and grapes grown in the summer garden.) When we finish this appetizer, all the moms will jump up and clear it away and start bringing in the mashed potatoes sprinkled with parsley picked outside the kitchen door, steaming gravy, and turkey grown by Uncle Doug and his twins and expertly carved by Grandpa. Next come parsnip patties, a specialty of the house; July-dried corn all creamed for Christmas; exquisite, light, melt-in-your-mouth rolls; homemade jellies and jams; pickles, carrots, cabbage coleslaw, cranberries, individual Christmas gelatin molds with fruit and whipped-cream topping, dressing, celery—there's more. Even after all these years we can't believe our eyes. Around the table goes the food, one person helping another until all plates are overflowing with food fit for a king.

The talk comes fast and the laughter rings out and little ones come to snuggle on moms' laps or play under the table. We retell our favorite Danish jokes, recount past memories, and build new ones as we sit, all feet under the same table, elbow-to-elbow, heart-to-heart. It's Christmas Day and we're all home again.

Everybody pitches in to clean up. Then there is time for a quick game of pool, or a family basketball game in which all ages are welcome on the court to shoot, pass, and dribble. Maybe we'll run to the Red Point for family sledding down the dump hill before the sun sets. The parents load up all the children, bundled in mittens, warm coats, and hats, for a weapons-carrier ride to the Red Point and some serious sledding. You'll love the weapons carrier left over from World War II; Grandpa restored it to carry tons of people to fun times. Pile in the sleds. Pile in the people. When you reach the top of the hill you'll see cousins jump on sleds two by two or one on top of another for the swift ride down the slope. Few make it to the bottom unscathed. There will be crashes into sagebrush and boys and girls, large and small, tumbling into each other as they fall off. What fun! Everyone laughs, some whimper a bit, but all jump up and go again. It's a reckless bunch. Soon you will be one of them, recounting the raucous adventures.

Night falls. The lights come on the garlands and wreaths adorning the front of the lovely and loved old home. The Christmas tree is lit and it is time for The Program! Children have prepared through music lessons all year for The Program (or wish they had). Paul sings, and Holly plays the piano, as do Adam, Aaron, Nathan, Scott, David, Darren, and Tom. Jon plays cello, Melissa plays harp, James and Taylor play violin accompanied by Lincoln, Justen plays banjo, Stephen is on mandolin, and Brad plays trumpet. It's a wonderful program—lots of variety and some "polish"—and it ends with the Myers family harmonizing. All do well and are applauded wildly.

For a reward, out come the presents. And it's chaos! One year, all of a sudden it started to become quieter. For, one by one, as the gifts were opened, we began to realize that Grandma had made a quilt for each child. Everyone was amazed at her handiwork and her love. Sleeping under the Christmas tree with cousins was extra cozy that year and for many seasons to come. Still, today, no one can believe all those quilts!

Years ago, The Program was quite short. Then each year more children were born, and gradually they began to participate. The beginners advanced. Now we see real progress. Children are performing for others, accompanying the singing at church, even playing on stage with the symphony. It's amazing what can come from a simple beginning in a family.

Now it is time for the sweet and sacred part, little baby. We read the Christmas story, acting out the parts. This year you will be the baby Jesus, the center of attention, just as all day the

Savior's sweet love has added savor to all we have done. In our Christmas pageant there will be an angel, of course, announcing the glad tidings of great joy. The shepherds will come with sheep who baaa. There will be wise men who will lay gifts before the baby Jesus, child of Mary and the Son of God, as Joseph keeps loving, tender watch. In a few years you can be a lamb. When you grow bigger you can be Joseph or a wise man in the pageant (and in life).

We will kneel together before day's end to praise God, to thank him for the gracious gift of his Only Begotten Son, who lived to show us the way and died to make it possible. We all know that he lives again and desires to help us do our best with his gift to us. Here is a humble group of people, a family, all bound together in love and trying to live to make those ties eternal. It is all because of Christmas that we can have such a glorious hope. Our own missionaries are absent today to teach that to others far away. Our lives are united in that common knowledge.

Now, precious little gift from God, you start a new generation. You have much to look forward to, beginning with Christmas. And because of Christmas you can return again one day to the loving arms of Jesus where so recently you rested.

Merry, merry Christmas, Murphy. Welcome to our world!

With lots of love,

Grandpa and Grandma Nadauld

Christmas Lessons

ELDER ALBERT CHOULES JR.

I learned early in my life that Christmas was a family affair. I remember what a thrill it was when I was old enough to help my parents with preparations for the younger children on Christmas Eve. I would go to bed with my brother and lie still until he went to sleep, then quietly slip out of bed. I felt so grown-up, and loved my parents for treating me as if I were. The next morning I acted very surprised at all the presents. I learned that Christmastime was giving time. In Depression years I saw parents give much to children and keep little for themselves. When I became a parent I understood that better.

A few years ago my brother and my sisters and I visited our childhood home. One of the first things we pointed out to each other was the spot where we used to put the Christmas tree. We were suddenly back several decades in fond memories. Childhood Christmas experiences seem to stay with us forever.

My first Christmas away from home was in Texas, where I was serving in the United States Marine Corps. I missed my family and friends. I was only eighteen and in a very different environment, a long way from home.

One of the married Marines invited me to his home off the base for Christmas dinner. I had never experienced Christmas celebrations that included liquor, but luckily the thoughtful family had provided some alcohol-free eggnog for me. They knew. As I reminisced about home and family and many previous Christmas experiences in faraway Idaho, I learned that family teachings can surface and influence us even when our family is far away. Teachings of righteous parents will support us. The whisperings of the Spirit are ever ready to be heeded; we will be blessed and enjoy life more if we listen to them.

Later, when I was married and our children came along, we began a Christmas Eve family tradition of reading the story of the birth of Jesus from the book of Luke. In the early years it was my opportunity to read to the children. As they grew and learned to read, we thrilled to hear their young voices share the sacred story. Discussing the Christ child took our thoughts from the

Christmas tree and the gifts to what was behind them.

As our children got older, the discussions became more mature. Each family member became a teacher as well as a learner. Our feelings about Christmas and the Savior became more and more meaningful as we mingled our thoughts and experiences.

Now our children have established their own families and homes. They have built upon their background and formed their own traditions, adding to and expanding on childhood memories. Undoubtedly the next generation will add even more as family traditions evolve and families and times change. But as we watch our children teach *their* children, we realize they learned more from family traditions than we thought they were absorbing. I learned early that it isn't the size of the gift or the expectation of it that is important or even very lasting. The love that accompanies the giving lasts long after the gift itself has disappeared. That love builds on other manifestations of love and sustains and supports when needs arise.

The three Christmases my wife, Marilyn, and I had in Germany were choice in many ways. We were introduced to the advent custom, wherein not only on Christmas Eve, but on the four Sunday evenings before it, the family gathers for a discussion of Christ and Christmas. That kind of weekly family home evening centered around the Savior leads to a more spiritual Christmas.

As an additional family activity one of those Christmases, we made a video of the children in our neighborhood, asking them not to tell their parents. Each child described his or her most memorable Christmas. The children—from the United States, Germany, Portugal, Sweden, Austria, and Australia—shared some very interesting thoughts. At a Christmas open house we showed the video to their parents, nourishing the family love that was already evident.

I learned to appreciate customs and traditions in a different country. I learned time and again that we are all Heavenly Father's children, and I felt his love for all. I felt the love of friends from different lands and shared their love of Jesus Christ. As they sang carols of Jesus' birth in their native tongues, I knew over and over that we are brothers and sisters in very deed. How tightly the gospel binds us together! What a blessing the binding is!

Christmastime is family time: a time to show love in our families and to draw closer to our heavenly family. It is a time not only to read the Christmas story, but to increase our resolve to better follow the Savior and his desires for us. At Christmas we celebrate the birth of the Savior, but the real story of Christmas includes also his life, death, and resurrection. He was born to give his life for us, to give us immortality and the opportunity for eternal life. As we think about and teach our families about Christmas, let us teach them the full story—from Bethlehem to Calvary and the Garden Tomb. Let us help them form their Christmas traditions, centered on Christ and filled with gratitude for what he did for us and what we can do for him in return.

On that first Christmas day Jesus was the gift from Heavenly Father. Later he was the giver, as he gave his life for all of us. His was the greatest gift, demonstrating an abundance of love for us all that can never be surpassed.

Christ's gift was his life. Our gift is our lives—lived in accordance with his gospel plan, keeping his commandments and honoring sacred covenants, with one goal: to come unto him eternally.

This lesson learned is the summation of them all. The Christ child was born on that first Christmas Day. Mary was his mother and he was the Only Begotten of our Heavenly Father. He was and is the Redeemer of us all, the Savior of the world. He lived and died for us. He lives today and heads his church, which bears his name. He began the restoration of it when he appeared with God our Father to the boy Joseph Smith. Because of all of this we can live again with them in the eternal realms. Just as Christmas is for families so is eternity. My prayer for us all is that we will live here in such a way that we can be assured of a family affair in the eternities.

The Best Christmas Ever

ELDER HUGH W. PINNOCK

From my early childhood I remember a tradition that developed quite by itself—at least it seemed to pop up and to just keep growing.

I suppose I was seven or eight years old when one Christmas seemed more special than any I had yet experienced. After a happy day spent with family and friends I crept into my parents' bedroom and said, in the most mature manner I could, "Thank you, Mom and Dad—this was the best Christmas ever." They acknowledged my gratitude with some kind words and I scooted off to bed.

It seemed like half a millennium before the next Christmas arrived. It too was a wonderful day. That was the year, if I remember correctly, that I received a Red Ryder BB gun and a chemistry set. Bedtime came too soon! Recalling the year before, and reflecting on how this one seemed even better, I again walked into my parents' room and blurted out something like, "Thank you for the best Christmas ever."

The next year I received skis, which I never learned to master, and books, which were becoming my favorite possessions. Friends were in and out of our home all day long. *Surely this is the best Christmas of all,* I thought, so I repeated the experiences of the two preceding Christmases by slipping into my parents' room after the lights were off and thanking them for "the best Christmas ever."

Each year seemed to be truly the best ever, and so the tradition continued up until I left for my mission. That year the mail from a loving family, the kindness of Church members, the goodness of a mission president and his family, and the excitement of investigators made my first Christmas away from home "the best Christmas ever." Another Christmas away with new investigators, added responsibility, and thoughtful remembrances from home became the newest "best ever."

College, marriage, military, children, Church callings, new blessings all made life more complicated, yet as each year would inevitably wind down it still seemed that each Christmas was the "best one ever."

We now have five married children with families of their own, or soon to have babies to bless their homes. Our youngest is serving a mission in Barcelona, Spain. We live nine thousand miles away from most of them. Now the packages we send seem to mean so much more than gifts we receive. Many new traditions have been woven into the fabric of our lives and our Christmases. Yet we acknowledge, with tears slipping down our faces, that these new blessings seem to testify that each new Christmas is "the best one of all."

Christmas Riches during Lean Years

ELDER HAROLD G. HILLAM

The cold Chicago wind caught my coat as I walked from the parking lot to the dental school. What can you expect right on the shores of Lake Michigan in late November? I was thinking about Christmas, our Christmas. We weren't going home this year, and it would be our first without the traditions of either Carol's home or mine. For three years we had made the trek along the icy roads of Iowa and Nebraska, across Wyoming's snow fields, and into either Idaho's or Utah's winter to spend Christmas with our families. This year we were short of both funds and courage to face that long, treacherous Highway 30.

Linda, our only child at that time, was two now, and we had decided to stay in Chicago and start our own traditions. Now, as the holidays approached, I wondered how it would be. No doubt a little low on the gift side, anyway; it was quite bare under the tree. How would we celebrate with only three people? Most of our close friends were heading west for the holidays, and several families in the ward were going elsewhere for the vacation.

December came before I knew it. Every day when I arrived home from school Christmas carols were playing, and often I could smell good things baking. I would get a taste, but the rest was for Christmas. You would have thought we were expecting a crowd. Three people were not many to eat all those goodies. Carol's mom had always had lots of special things to eat around the holidays—I was reaping the benefits of that tradition.

Carol, a schoolteacher, was involved in Christmas art projects and decorations. She was also busy planning the Christmas musical program for the school, which was a little tricky with a student body that was two-thirds Jewish. They hadn't had a Christmas program in previous years, but she got around the problem with a chorus she started in the school. They had presented a Hanukkah program with the Christian children participating, so it seemed only natural that the Jewish students should sing in the Christmas musical. All these wonderful December involvements spilled a Christmas spirit over into my world—which as usual was filled with case studies, heavy medical reading assignments, patients' needs, and tedious preparations for finals.

Our other Christmases had been filled with the excitement of going home, knowing the Christmas spirit would be there waiting for us when we arrived. This year we were making it happen each December day. I was in the bishopric, and we had been working with a less-active family. Why not invite them to spend some time with us on Christmas—maybe Christmas Eve? Carol thought it was a great idea. We could have a dinner on Christmas Eve. That way, if they had plans for Christmas Day, this party would not interfere. We were delighted when they accepted.

During the early part of December we went shopping—or rather, looking. We thought it would give little Linda a feeling of the season, and she could see Santa. Actually, the stores were beautiful, and when you have no money to spend it is even better because there are no decisions—just enjoyment. Linda loved all the wonderful toys, dolls, and stuffed animals. There was a festive air about the whole experience.

When it got nearer to Christmas, we looked for a tree. Each week they got a little cheaper, and that was fine with me, because I wasn't used to paying. In our family we were accustomed to cutting our own tree. We often selected it during the summer months on fishing trips, and returned to cut it down the day after Thanksgiving, before the heavy snow fell. We put the tree into a bucket of water outside near the house to preserve it. Then on Christmas Eve we set it up undecorated in our living room. That night Santa would come and decorate our tree. We were the luckiest kids in the neighborhood, I thought, feeling sorry for all the children who had to decorate their own trees. Waking up Christmas morning and seeing the beautiful tree was one of my childhood thrills.

Carol had never heard of such a tradition, and wanted to decorate the tree to bring a little spirit of the holidays into our home. It was probably just as well, because the tree place threw in some extra branches that we could use in decorating the house. The only formal decorations we had were lights and balls that our parents no longer needed in their color-coordinated decorations. I found that I had to use a bit of magic on the tree, drilling holes in the trunk to add extra branches for balance. I left the tree for Linda and Carol to decorate while I studied.

After some time, Linda knocked at the door to our bedroom, where we had squeezed in a desk for studying. She wanted me to see her tree. As she opened the door, I could hear the music playing, and I could smell popcorn popping. I was amazed at the creation of beauty that had developed out of very little, but mostly I was lifted to see how happy our daughter was. This was her Christmas tree. She and I sat for a long time watching the lights and eating popcorn.

We read stories each night to Linda as part of her going-to-bed ritual, and of course during the month of December these were Christmas stories. As Christmas approached, my wife and daughter seemed to be working on something else, but I was too involved with finals and papers to sort it all out.

We had decided not to buy gifts for ourselves, but rather to spend what little money we had on something for our daughter. A baby doll and a little bed in the window of Shopper's World barely fit that budget. Carol took one of her party dresses from college days and made it over into a beautiful Christmas dress for Linda. A box arrived from our parents containing some gifts to put under the tree. We were appreciative because it gave our daughter something to open along with the few simple items we had wrapped. Our house was beginning to look like Christmas, sound like Christmas, and smell like Christmas.

The day I finished finals—several days before Christmas Eve—out came all the good things Carol had been making all December. We carefully placed them on decorated paper plates and gave them to our neighbors and friends. Linda thought that was wonderful as long as we saved some for home. She giggled and laughed at each house and occasionally sang "Jingle Bells." This activity, such a great change from school, warmed our spirits.

Christmas Eve arrived and Carol prepared a turkey dinner for our guests and us. She wanted this dinner to be formal—at least, as formal as we could make it. It was festive and beautiful, with rich color and tasty food. After dinner my wife announced that we had a program. That was a surprise! I realized that perhaps this was what she and Linda had been planning all month. We settled in around the lighted tree for the performance.

Carol brought in a box on which Linda placed a cardboard nativity set borrowed from the ward Primary, and they began. "And it came to pass in those days, that there went out a decree from Caesar Augustus, that all the world should be taxed. . . . And all went to be taxed, every one into his own city. And Joseph also went up from Galilee, out of the city of Nazareth, into Judaea, unto the city of David, which is called Bethlehem; (because he was of the house and lineage of David:) To be taxed with Mary his espoused wife, being great with child." (Luke 2:1–5.) As the words continued to fall from Linda's lips (with occasional help from her mom), I was thrilled. This was my little two-and-a-half-year-old girl telling me the reason for our Christmas celebration as found in the book of Luke. As she came to each character, she pointed them out in the Primary nativity scene. Every now and then she would stop and we would all sing a Christmas carol appropriate for that scene. As the story reached the end my wife read more, with Linda filling in words here and there, but I knew she knew the real meaning of Christmas. Could there be a better gift for me?

I'm not sure our guests were as thrilled as I was, or as touched, though they enjoyed our time together and spoke of it often. Light snow was falling when we opened the door to bid them good night and Merry Christmas. As I closed the door, I could see that Linda was placing the nativity scene under the tree. "I thought that baby Jesus looked good under the tree with the pretty presents," she said. *He certainly does,* I thought, for I had felt his presence that evening.

Linda was soon off to bed, and we brought out her little doll and doll bed from their hiding spot to place under the tree. Carol and I stood hand in hand looking at our Christmas tree, thinking of our December, and feeling the presences of that beautiful time of year. We were rich.

Years have passed since that Christmas with just our family of three. Six more children have been added to our family, and we have continued the Christmas Eve tradition of beginning our celebration with Christ. We dress in our best clothes and have a wonderful dinner, often with guests to share our table. The cardboard figures in the nativity scene have been replaced by our own children acting out the parts. Everything is ready for Christmas Day, the hustle and bustle is over, and it is time to remember and appreciate the greatest gift ever given man, which had its earthly beginning in a manger in Bethlehem.

It is often in the lean years that we discover our greatest riches. We have photographed our family nativity scene for thirty-three years now, and each time I remember how it all started, when a little two-year-old girl placed a borrowed cardboard nativity scene under a very simple tree with just a few presents. And as I remember, the warmth of His presence still warms my heart every Christmas Eve.

Christmas Giving

ELDER GENE R. COOK

The word *Christmas* might be divided into two words. Those who understand Spanish as well as English know that with a mixture of Spanish and English, *Christmas* could mean "more Christ." To me, the perfect Christmas would be more of Christ and less of many of the other things we tend to associate with the season.

Most of us spend a lot of time in the weeks before Christmas moving through many stores, looking for presents. What do we see? A lot of things that make people happy, especially children, right? I have seen automatic trains, small cars, rifles, pistols, dolls, all kinds of toys and expensive games. I have seen microwave ovens, automatic dishwashers, televisions, radios, VCRs, even satellite dishes—a little of everything—and I ask, are these real gifts? We can easily get lost in all this and lose the real meaning of Christmas, pressured to buy something *tangible* and give it to someone else. Such buying, done in the right spirit, is part of Christmas, but I want to talk about something deeper.

When I think about Christmas as a Latter-day Saint, I turn to the scriptures with this question in mind: "What would Jesus Christ do?" What would he *give* if he were here today? If he taught one thing more than anything else, it was to give, give, give, and give, even as he gave his own life. Try thinking of Christ and Christmas as you consider these passages of scripture that emphasize the word *give:*

"I am the good shepherd: the good shepherd *giveth* his life for the sheep." (John 10:11.)

What would the Father say on Jesus' birthday? He might say: "For God so loved the world, that he *gave* his only begotten Son, that whosoever believeth in him should not perish, but have everlasting life." (John 3:16.)

To his disciples, Christ said: "Heal the sick, cleanse the lepers, raise the dead, cast out devils: freely ye have received, freely *give*." (Matthew 10:8.)

"For unto whomsoever much is *given*, of him shall be much required: and to whom men have committed much, of him they will ask the more." (Luke 12:48.)

Here is a great principle to consider when giving a gift: "If a man being evil *giveth* a gift, he doeth it grudgingly; wherefore it is counted unto him the same as if he had retained the gift; wherefore he is counted evil before God." (Moroni 7:8.)

"For God loveth a cheerful *giver*." (2 Corinthians 9:7.)

I really like this last scripture, which summarizes it all: "It is more blessed to *give* than to receive." (Acts 20:35.)

I declare in the name of Jesus Christ that he gave all and did not think of receiving anything. It truly touches me to think about Christmas and about giving.

What will be the greatest gift of all? I think that the greatest and most difficult gifts to give are those of our time, our talents, and ourselves.

Some years ago when we lived in Peru our family decided that we wanted to improve our Christmases. After studying the scriptures and understanding the meaning of giving the best we could, we set some guidelines for the Cook family. We were determined to follow these simple guidelines to try to better our Christmas that year:

1. We would try not to buy anything for each other from a store.

2. The presents that we would give would be made with our own hands. We would give of our time to the ones we loved.

3. Regarding our homemade gifts, we could not purchase any materials with which to make them. We had to use materials already on hand within our home. (This constituted a great challenge.)

4. We were to find the best way to give of our time, our talents, and ourselves, to truly involve ourselves in giving to others.

Some interesting things happened that Christmas. First, one of our young sons decided to make a key holder for Mother's keys. We had many keys but nowhere to put them and they frequently got mixed up. What a mess it was! We decided that a holder would be an excellent gift for Mom.

We began by looking for a piece of wood. I wanted to buy it, but my son reminded me that we couldn't. Let me tell you that we spent an hour getting a little piece of wood ready that would have taken us minutes to buy. When we tried to sand it, we realized that we didn't have anything to sand it with. So we had to invent a way to sand it, and we did.

We soon came up against the problem of painting the wood. Fortunately, we had a little yellow paint in the house, but we were stuck without a paintbrush. Again I thought of going to the store, but my son said: "Dad, someone had to invent the paintbrush. How did he do it?" We made a paintbrush by pulling some straw out of my wife's broom, and though I had my doubts about how it would work, I can tell you sincerely that we made a brush as excellent as the best brush in any store.

We then had a problem with the hooks for the keys. We solved that problem by bending nails in the shape of hooks, doing each with love and lots of patience. And on Christmas morning, this young boy had a delightful experience as he gave his mother a true gift from his heart. We still have that key holder after all these years.

One daughter found a rock, painted it with the same yellow paint (since it was all we had), and wrote on it: "Mom, I love you." We still have that, too—a rock prepared with pure love.

Another son made a llama with straw also pulled from the broom. (Poor broom, it almost disappeared.) This boy, our eldest, really created a quality item. It probably would have sold well in any store in Peru. Interestingly enough, I add again, we still have it today.

If you're not able to make something by hand, how about offering "gift certi-cates" for services? These can be given anonymously to neighbors, indicating things such as: "The snow in the front of your house will be shoveled all this week by neighborhood 'angels,'" or "We lov-ingly owe you two lawn mowings," or "This certificate is good for two loaves of homemade bread." Such gifts warm the heart of the giver sometimes even more than that of the receiver.

We have enjoyed giving gift certifi-cates to family members. Some examples are: "I will make your bed seven times," from one child to another, or "I will do the dishes three times." Mother likes this one: "Six hours of peace and harmony."

To my mother, who lives far away, I gave a certificate promising to send twelve letters, one each month in the coming year. This gift to her was better than anything I could have bought in a store because it showed more profound love, more giving of myself. As I evaluate what Christ gave, I always come to the conclusion that he really gave of himself time and time again. In his own manner he gave the best gifts a person could give.

If I were to summarize what a person might do to have a great Christmas, I would suggest:

1. I will do acts of charity for others.

2. I will seek to give of myself spiritu-ally to others.

3. I will find someone to help and to pray for.

4. I will secretly fast for someone who has a problem.

5. As an offering to God, I will find someone who really needs a blessing and provide it.

6. I will extend my love to all.

7. I will comfort the sick.

8. I will visit widows and the home-less and share with them the scriptures.

9. I will sing with someone who needs to sing.

These will be real gifts, to give as Jesus gave of himself. As I understand things, this is the true evidence of Christ being among us. In the last days, the King will say:

"Ye blessed of my Father, inherit the kingdom prepared for you from the foun-dation of the world:

"For I was an hungred, and ye gave me meat: I was thirsty, and ye gave me drink: I was a stranger, and ye took me in:

"Naked, and ye clothed me: I was sick, and ye visited me: I was in prison, and ye came unto me.

"Then shall the righteous answer him, saying, Lord, when saw we thee an hungred, and fed thee? or thirsty, and gave thee drink?

"When saw we thee a stranger, and took thee in? or naked, and clothed thee?

"Or when saw we thee sick, or in prison, and came unto thee?

"And the King shall answer and say unto them, Verily I say unto you, Inasmuch as ye have done it unto one of the least of these my brethren, ye have done it unto me." (Matthew 25:34–40.)

I testify to you of the Savior Jesus Christ, the King of all the world, a divine being, the one who truly has all power in heaven and on earth, who has given us such a great example that it cannot be ignored. He is one of our brothers who has told us that he will call us not servants, but friends. Let us look within ourselves so that we may become like him. When we have his fellowship, we will think about him, and as we let our desires and actions be like his, we will become like him.

President David O. McKay said it well: "That man is truly great who is most Christlike. What you sincerely think in your heart of Jesus Christ will determine what you are and will largely determine what your acts will be." By choosing Jesus Christ as our ideal, we create within ourselves a desire to be like him.

I declare with confidence, faith, full knowledge, and peace that Jesus is the Son of God, the Redeemer of the world, our personal Savior. May we honor him at Christmas and always, and may our actions demonstrate our deep faith in him.

Peace on Earth

ELDER F. BURTON HOWARD

Sometimes, when cares of the day press heavily
    upon our minds,
We long for the tranquility of days gone by.
Sometimes in troubled sleep comes a peace,
    foreign to this day and time,
When the past lives again and carefree days of youth and
    home return
To mock the studied purposes of the present.

At such times we reflect upon the efforts of men, who,
    by careful application of their energies,
Seek to recapture the simplicity of an earlier life—
And we wonder if we, too, would not find some greater
    happiness by retreating from this world;
By forsaking the pride, the contestings and compulsions
    of this century,
And adopting the customs and mores of those who lived
    close to the land.

But the answer always comes, clear and compelling—
You, the children of a troubled age, must face the uncertainties
    of your time with head held high.
Your hope of peace must not be based on that which prompts
    escape or fear.

Only your heritage of peace lies in the past.
The precious serenity you seek must be wrought from a
    present world without compromise, without concession.

Only thus can you with honor find peace—
Only peace with honor is peace at all.
So will it ever be.

Our Last California Christmas

ELDER JOHN K. CARMACK

You know how all things can seem to be set, moving along a path ordained by choices and circumstances, and then an unforeseen and unchosen change swiftly reverses everything. Life's energy moves you in a new, almost opposite direction, and looking back you see the pivot, an about-face on a silent order barked by an unseen sergeant.

In my boyhood such an about-face for my family followed a day etched in my memory—December 7, 1941. The silent order that followed Pearl Harbor moved our family to California as a part of the vast energy unleashed by the winds of World War II.

My wife, Shirley, and I met, courted, and married in Westwood, California, home for many who were drawn to this Los Angeles suburb by the temple or by the stimulating community built around the UCLA campus. We both did our graduate work at UCLA and decided to stay because we loved Westwood and the warm, energetic, and self-confident people who made the west side of Los Angeles their home. Several times we had almost left for smaller communities,

enticed by attractive job offers, but something held us in Westwood. We finally decided that this was our home and probably would always be so.

Yes, at times we longed for a smaller community, less traffic, and a simpler life. Shirley especially often felt like a chauffeur trying to help our family meet all of its challenges and activities; and civic, church, family, and professional life gobbled up most of our time. We barely had time to breathe.

We concluded, however, that that was the way we were, and that a change in geography wouldn't change our own nature. Besides, life had been good to us. We enjoyed a full, exciting, and meaningful lifestyle that revolved around our home. With a few adjustments we would live out our days here and be thankful.

As Christmas of 1980 approached things seemed to be going better and better. Our older children were in college, and new professional opportunities we had hoped for came to us, promising an easier life. We had built a comfortable new home that we envisioned would be the center of family life for the rest of our days. We enjoyed good health and a measure of prosperity and peace. Business associates seemed able to shoulder more of the professional responsibilities we shared, leaving us more freedom.

An especially meaningful experience heightened our anticipation of Christmas that year. Shirley sang with the Southern California Mormon Choir and I was its priesthood adviser. In November we traveled to Israel on a long-awaited concert tour with the choir, performing in Jerusalem, Tel Aviv, and several kibbutzim in the countryside. In addition, we visited the Sea of Galilee, Capernaum, Nazareth, the Israel-Lebanon border, the Golan Heights, and the historical places of Jerusalem.

We prepared our hearts for Christmas by singing "O Little Town of Bethlehem" while seated on the hills overlooking Bethlehem. Sheep grazed nearby, watched over by shepherds, much as depicted in the New Testament Christmas story. In Bethlehem, Shirley carefully selected figures carved from local olive wood, depicting the first Christmas. Our family Christmas was a cherished tradition and we especially looked forward to welcoming Lisa, Paula, and Stanford home for the holidays and rejoining Barbara and Julia.

At the end of November we went by appointment to Security Pacific Bank in Westwood and paid off our last debt—a loan secured by a deed of trust against our home. We had achieved a family goal of being debt free at last.

Then we prepared for Christmas. We selected a large tree for our living room and, as usual, Shirley presided over the arrangement of lights and decorations in our home. We added the manger scene newly acquired in Bethlehem.

Then, on December sixteenth, all things changed for us. I was in the office that day digging out from under the pile of accumulated work on my desk. At noon I took the elevator to the bottom floor of the office building, where officers and board members of the Western Los Angeles Regional Chamber of Commerce were gathered for a Christmas buffet and party. I carefully selected my favorite holiday foods from the beautiful spread on the conference room table and was about to enjoy the luncheon when I was called to the telephone. "Arthur Haycock, President Spencer W. Kimball's personal executive secretary, just called and asked me to find you," my secretary announced.

"I'll be right up," I said. I left my plate on the table, little realizing that I would never return to enjoy Christmas lunch.

The urgency of the request disquieted me. I took a deep breath and picked up the telephone. Arthur apologized, "Sorry to get you out of your meeting, but since we are going to change your life we thought you wouldn't mind." Next he began gathering information about the number and ages of our children. Suddenly he said, "Just a minute, President Kimball wants to speak to you." That familiar voice came over the line, with the quiet hoarseness that had become so powerful to the Saints. We first exchanged family greetings. I told him how much I had enjoyed his article in the December *Ensign,* in which he recounted a special Christmas with Sister Kimball and Elder and Sister Howard W. Hunter on the hills of Judea overlooking Bethlehem. Then he dropped the bombshell. "We would like to call you into full-time Church service as a mission president. Will you accept? Can you arrange your affairs to leave for three years? Do you need to talk to Sister Carmack? Will your business partners let you go? Tell them they will be blessed. Do you speak any languages other than English? Thank you very much, Brother Carmack. We will send you a letter."

Then I was alone. I couldn't bring myself to go back to the Chamber luncheon. Instinctively I dialed home, finding Shirley there. "Are you alone? Are you sitting down? President Kimball just called," I said. We slept little and talked much that night.

Theoretically we would be back home again in three years. Something deep inside, however, told me that this would be the last Christmas in our California home. We wanted to share the news with our children in an intimate family setting, alone and without outside distractions. Easier said than done. With all the excitement and bustle of shopping, Christmas parties and programs, and friends dropping in, we couldn't find a moment. Finally we simply set a time one night for the family to gather. This event was as pivotal for the children as for us—with far-reaching consequences for all.

Quietly we shared the fateful news. This Christmas would be our last one here for at least three years. We were going on a mission. Reaction was immediate and varied, from uncontrollable

sobs to quiet contemplation. We were all in shock with the news that had changed everything, it seemed. Of course, the important things could never be changed, except by us. We were sealed together eternally as a family, transcending even earthly boundaries and certainly making geography secondary.

Things quickly jelled. Lisa became engaged to Brian Palmer during the first hour of New Year's Day as they walked in formal clothing on the Santa Monica beach. Paula would complete her undergraduate work, then accept employment in Washington, D.C. Stanford would be ready for his mission at nearly the same time we would start ours, and would accompany us for two weeks to Boise, Idaho (where we were later assigned), before departing for the MTC and Bolivia. Barbara and Julia, then ages eleven and thirteen, would become Idaho girls, enjoying the wonderful environment and traditions of Boise.

No wonder we had such a wonderful, intense, yet fearsome Christmas as we clung to our memories, traditions, home, and friends in 1980. Looking back we can see that in many ways it was our best Christmas as well as the last in our California home.

On the first Christmas, Jesus left his home and his high and holy station with the Father to be born of Mary in a manger in Bethlehem. Everything pivots on that day, even the calendar. The consequences were eternally far reaching and awe inspiring. We celebrate that birth with gifts, Christmas carols, lights, and family gatherings. We sing, "Glory to God in the highest, and on earth peace, good will toward men." The Savior came in a lowly manger, without status or fanfare except as provided by the signs and angels announcing his birth. He did not hesitate, but voluntarily accepted his role. In a small way, we better understood what Christmas was all about on that last Christmas in our California home.

Lessons of True Sharing

ELDER LLOYD P. GEORGE

Christmas is a time for reflection, a time to worship and give thanks, a time of remembering. Especially at this time we give thanks to a kind, loving Father in Heaven for his plan of redemption, which if followed will bring eternal life. We thank him also for his omniscient wisdom in allowing us our agency to learn lessons that will prepare us for the eternities.

We are taught that "God so loved the world, that he gave his only begotten Son, that whosoever believeth in him should not perish, but have everlasting life." (John 3:16.) Only in giving that which matters most are we, too, justified and blessed. True sharing involves giving the better part of ourselves to bless the lives of others. We may find it comparatively easy to give of our knowledge, our wealth, and our blessings; it takes a greater effort and commitment to share things that are scarce to us. Nonetheless, it is only through this greater effort that we are brought to the throne of God.

A poem by James R. Lowell, "The Vision of Sir Launfal," tells an interesting story of a young knight who rode out into the world in search of the Holy Grail (the cup from which the Master supposedly drank at the Last Supper). He dedicated his life to the quest. He was young, handsome, and strong, clothed in bright and shining armor, mounted on a gallant white charger. As he crossed the drawbridge riding out into the world, a leper put up his hand to him, begging alms. The young knight reached into his pouch, took out a gold coin, and flung it to the beggar as he rode on. He really did not give the beggar very much, because no one would accept even a gold coin from a leper.

The young knight searched for the cup in vain, spending his life in the quest. Finally he returned to his castle, shrunken with age. His armor was no longer bright, his mount no longer a charger but just a tired, old, gray horse. As he was about to cross the drawbridge into the castle, once again the leper put up his hand begging for alms. This time Sir Launfal stopped, got down from his horse, reached into his knapsack, and took out the only thing he had—a crust of bread. He then dipped his own cup into the stream and gave the crust of bread and cup of cold water to the beggar.

The wooden cup from which the beggar drank turned into the Holy Grail for which the knight had searched! The miracle was that this time the beggar was fed and nourished by Sir Launfal's ability to share all that he had, rather than just effortlessly flipping a coin. The beggar then said an interesting thing:

> *Not what we give, but what we share.*
> *For the gift without the giver is bare;*
> *Who gives himself with his alms feeds three,*
> *Himself, his hungering neighbor, and me.*

A few years ago my daughter, with her family of ten children, learned the valuable principle of sharing because of an economic crisis. May I share her story with you in her own words:

"Christmastime is the best time of the year for making memories, especially for children. Thanks to my precious six-year-old son, Ben, a memory was made several years ago that I will cherish forever.

"As Christmas drew near, my heart and mind were uneasy. Truly I was dreading the prospects of the upcoming season. With the economy falling and money scarce, our finances were just not what they had been in the past. The children (ten of them under the age of fourteen) had been busy making their lists for Santa. Christmases in the past had included for each child seven or eight small gifts plus one special, more expensive gift. Ben had seen a car in the toy store that he really wanted for his special gift. The little girls had their lists made, which included mostly clothes and jewelry. The little boys wanted various toys and games they had seen advertised on TV.

"Because funds were limited, we decided that this year we would be able to get each child only one item—but if possible we would try to make it the special gift on his or her list. We talked to the children and explained that Christmas this year would be a little different. The five older children understood, and the ones younger than Ben didn't know the difference between a two-dollar and a twenty-dollar gift anyway.

"Christmas Eve finally arrived. Everyone was excited and the little ones speculated about what Santa's pack would have in store for them. We had our traditional Christmas party, starting with a buffet supper in the living room and ending with the family acting out the Christmas story. The part of baby Jesus was played by the newest member of the family—a role that, I might add, was generally held for only a year at our house. We talked about Christ, his great example, and what his birth means to us all. The children put a snack out for Santa and then surveyed the house to decide where he should leave their presents. Ben spoke for the corner at the end of the fireplace. He got his stocking, laid it carefully on his spot, and proclaimed, 'This is where Santa is going to put my stack of presents.' My heart skipped a beat. He had one gift—the Transformer car he had requested. Oh, I hoped he wouldn't be too disappointed.

"Christmas morning came early, as it usually does for mothers. We walked together down the hallway before entering the living room. For just a brief second, I too wanted to believe in Santa. I wanted to believe that he had made a visit after the house was quiet and left every child that special stack of presents.

"We entered the living room and the excitement began. All the children went straight to their treasures, and the ribbons and paper began to fly. Their screams of pleasure and delight filled the air as they opened their gifts. I watched as Ben went to his corner and checked out his little present sitting there all by itself. I can still remember, as clearly as if it were yesterday, how he jumped up and down and giggled with delight as he anticipated what his gift might be. I expected him to say something about his single gift, but he never seemed to notice.

"I learned at that moment from a very special child what Christmas was all about. Instead of opening his gift, he ran to his little brothers and joined with them to share in their joy and excitement over their toys. He watched as all the other children opened their packages; his enthusiasm and delight for them caught me quite off guard. Why wasn't he opening his gift? Every now and then he would run back to the little present still sitting there in the corner, pick it up, and dance and jump around as though he couldn't wait to tear off the paper. Each time he would set it back down and join the others to figure out how this worked or how that fit together. He was so happy. He laughed and cheered and shared in everyone's joy. I watched in amazement. Who was this child who on Christmas Day had the least, but shared the most?

"Later, as the excitement began to die down a little, Ben picked up his present again, this time to open it. The look in his eyes let everyone know that that present was just for him! The paper came off and the shiny blue car inside was, he said, 'just what I wanted.' He ran from one to the other saying, 'Look what I got! Look what Santa brought just for me!'

"Yes, as a mother, I experienced something that Christmas Day that I will never forget: memories etched forever in my heart, a child full of love, full of caring, eager to share.

"The years have come and gone, and I often think about that day. With some curiosity, I've wondered what Ben's memories were of that Christmas of 1985. I recently asked Ben, now fourteen, if he could remember that Christmas when he got a blue car. He paused for just a second, and then a big smile lit up his face as he confirmed that it was indeed his best Christmas."

Had I known of my daughter's economic plight, I would have wanted to change it. Thus, unintentionally and unwittingly, I would have deprived this family of a valuable lesson in sharing the joy we have with others.

I am grateful that the Lord has allowed me this time and opportunity to share his precious way of life with his children, to share with others the love I feel he has for me and the mercy shown me in times of trial, and above all to testify "that he is, and that he is a rewarder of them that diligently seek him." (Hebrews 11:6.)

The Letters

E L D E R L . L I O N E L K E N D R I C K

When I was a young boy, listening to adults reminisce, forty years seemed like forever. At my present age I find it quite easy to remember, in vivid detail, events and experiences that took place forty years ago. Even the feelings and impressions associated with those experiences come flooding forth in almost the same fullness as when they were first felt.

About forty years ago, on December 11, 1954, I was baptized a member of the Church. At that time I was serving as an officer in the Air Force, attending Officer Personnel School at Scott Air Force Base near Belleville, Illinois. My wife, Myrtis, and I had one child, a son who was then nine months old.

That Christmas season of 1954 was the greatest and most special one that I had ever experienced. It was my first Christmas as a father and as a member of the Church. I knew that I had been given the greatest of all gifts that I had ever received. Yet perhaps I did not fully understand the extent and manner in which these grand gifts would shape my future and help to determine my divine destiny.

That Christmas season was a very tender time for me in other respects. I had received orders to be stationed in Japan, and it was uncertain if my family would be able to join me at a future time during my tour of duty there. This would be the first time in our married life that we would be apart from each other. The thought of not being with my wife and son was more than I wanted to experience. I still have vivid memories of telling them good-bye for an indefinite season of time. As it turned out, we would not see each other for five long months, which seemed to me to be an eternity.

I reported to Parks Air Force Base in California to process for my overseas assignment and to receive a flight schedule. While awaiting an assigned flight, I had time to reflect on the events of the past few weeks, and the extended time ahead away from my family. I thought of my new son and the special love that I had for him. I recalled those tender moments and experiences that we had had together during those few months since his birth. My heart filled with the joy that he had brought into our lives. How much I would miss him and his mother, and how I longed to be with them!

My thoughts turned to my baptism and the events that had led to it. My heart filled with gratitude for my wife, Myrtis, and for the great influence that she was as she lived the principles of the gospel while we were dating and after our marriage. I recalled in vivid detail the sweet, powerful testimony she bore to me that the Church was true. I also recalled her desire for me to be taught the gospel, but with the caution and counsel that I must never embrace it for her sake, but only when I had a witness that it was true. I could feel of the faith she had in me that I would follow her wise and loving counsel. She later shared with me that she had always "known" that I would accept the gospel.

My thoughts then turned to the first Sunday after our arrival in Belleville, Illinois. We attended the investigator's class in the Belleville Branch. Hal J. Coburn, a returned missionary and a fellow officer, was the teacher. The Spirit was strong as he taught and bore testimony; I had never felt before what I felt that day. I knew then that I had to know if the Church was true. The second Sunday, I experienced a further hunger and thirst to know the truth. I knew that I could not wait until the following Sunday to learn more about the gospel. I asked Brother Coburn, my marvelous teacher, if he and his wife, Peggy, could come to our apartment each Wednesday to teach me more of these wonderful

principles. He was excited to honor my request.

After studying the gospel almost non-stop from September to December, I experienced that peaceful and certain witness that the Church was true, and I had a great desire to be baptized. I will never forget that sacred experience. As I sat in my room at Parks Air Base, I re-lived the feeling that I had as I came from the waters of baptism on that wonderful December day in 1954. Shortly thereafter, I promised Heavenly Father that I would do whatever his servants asked me to do, and that I would be obedient and serve him faithfully to the best of my ability.

My thoughts moved from my baptism to the Christmas season we had just spent with our parents before my departure for Japan. We left Illinois the day after my baptism to travel to Louisiana to be with our family. It was a wonderful time in our lives. We spent special time with our new son and were thrilled to see his excitement over his first Christmas. Those wonderful feelings were sometimes broken by the realization that we would not be together for some time in the months ahead.

As I continued to ponder, I thought of my parents, who were not members of the Church. I had such tender feelings of gratitude for them for teaching me so well the principles of personal purity, obedience, integrity, love, and work. I was thrilled to think that they had taught me to live these true principles even before I found and accepted the gospel. I was grateful that I had followed their counsel and example.

As I thought of the joy of fatherhood

and how much I already missed my little son, Larry, I felt a strong impression of the Spirit to write him a letter. I wrote a long letter to be given to him at the appropriate time and age. In that letter, I expressed the tender and special love that I had for him. I bore my testimony of the truthfulness of the gospel and the spiritual feelings I had for the Church. I gave him his father's first counsel, sharing feelings close to my heart and expressing my hope that he, too, would acquire some of these same feelings and develop a strong and obedient character.

That letter has been special in his life as well as in mine. We both have retained copies of it over these past forty years. My son has followed that early counsel I gave him in the letter. He has been a great blessing in my life, along with our other children, Hal, Dana, and Merri Ellen, who were born under the covenant, as my wife and I were sealed in the Hawaii Temple on our way home from Japan.

During the time I was serving as a mission president, Larry wrote me a tender letter expressing his gratitude and feelings concerning the letter that I wrote to him in 1954. He included counsel that I have treasured. Now his letter to me is one of my prized possessions; it has been for me what my letter has been for him.

The Christmas season is indeed a glorious one. It's a time to remember our positive past. It's a time to recall and relive our special spiritual experiences, and to recognize our bountiful blessings. It's a time to review our accomplishments and rethink our priorities—to resolve to do better and to set goals and plans for such improvement. It's a time to repent and make needed corrections to stay on course on our return trip home to the presence of Heavenly Father. It's a time to reach out to others in selfless service. It's a time to renew our commitments and to respect the Lord's commandments and reverence his sacred covenants. It's a time to come to know him and to worship him in his holy house.

For me, the Christmas season will always be a time to remember and review the letters. As I search the sacred scriptures, I realize that these revered revelations are indeed letters to us from the Savior, whose divine desire is for each of us to return home safely. I will be eternally grateful to Heavenly Father for the experiences of forty Christmases ago, when I learned of these truths for myself.

The Real Christmas

ELDER RICHARD P. LINDSAY

The year 1933 had been a difficult one for our family. The previous winter my father had died suddenly, leaving my widowed mother with six young children, from four to fourteen years of age. Ten days after my father's death, my oldest brother, age fourteen, who was to be the new "head of the house," died unexpectedly from an acute illness.

The Depression, with all its demoralizing and devastating consequences to happy family life, continued to exact its toll of discouragement and frustration. Many of our neighbors, in the absence of employment, or with lifetime savings lost in failed banks, were unable to meet payments on their homes or to pay their taxes. My mother was struggling to save our home, where she and my father had moved immediately after their marriage and where the beginnings of a satisfying and blessed family life had begun.

Prior to marriage my mother had trained in Michigan to become a registered nurse. This was considered an unusual accomplishment for a Utah girl, especially when professional training was not offered in the state.

Unable, in this Depression year, to find regular employment to support her large family, my mother would accept jobs to do home nursing for families experiencing serious illnesses who were unable to afford regular hospital care. The fatigue from such efforts, combined with the responsibility of caring for her own family, brought her own health to the breaking point.

As a child, I wondered what else could happen to make life more difficult. In this otherwise discouraging setting, I remember seeing a relief truck parked in front of the elementary school across the street. It was loaded with fresh-dressed turkeys for distribution to needy families—those whose family heads were out of work.

I reported this happy development to my mother, who was ill and in bed. I felt that I had scouted out the answer to our Christmas feast, which would help alleviate the depressing circumstances in which our family had been placed.

My mother used the moment to impart a great principle, one that I have tried to retain throughout my life.

"Richard," she said, "we are not a poor family, we are just a family that has experienced some temporary misfortune. Those turkeys are for the people who *really* need them. We have a fine red rooster in the chicken coop, and you and your brother can help prepare him for a real Christmas dinner."

By present standards our family Christmas that year would be considered somber. The few Christmas gifts included largely clothing necessities and fresh fruit. The important ingredients for a great Christmas celebration were still in place, however. Our home was warm, and we had coal in the basement to last the winter. Mother's health was improving, and we had been able to pay our taxes on our home. In addition, I had saved a whole dollar from work projects I had been able to locate, and with that purchased thirteen presents for family members, including a twenty-five-cent bottle of "Italian Balm" for my mother.

On Christmas my mother expressed a prayer of thanks for the rich blessings our family had received, and prayed for those who were truly needy. In subsequent years when the material blessings of life have been more abundant, I have still reflected on the "real Christmas" of 1933.

This chapter appeared originally in *This People*, December/January 1985, pp. 39–40. Used by permission.

A Good Use for Fifty Dollars

BISHOP H. DAVID BURTON

Each holiday season we try to plan a family activity of some kind prior to Christmas. Sometimes it involves adults only; another time we may focus on the grandchildren; sometimes it is a whole-family event. Our memories include a sleigh ride followed by dinner; a meal at the Lion House and a Christmas play; a sleepover with a Christmas video, treats, and games for the grandchildren; a carriage ride downtown with Santa; a snow-mobile weekend at our cabin; a caroling party when we delivered a food basket to a homebound great-uncle; and a sub-for-Santa project.

For Christmas of 1993, we decided to try something different. At the beginning of December, we sent each of our children (married and those at home) a letter with fifty single dollar bills enclosed. The letter suggested they find a use for the money in helping someone else. The stipulations were that they would not spend it on themselves or any other member of our family, and that the use be anony-mous. They were to share their experiences, if they desired, at our traditional Christmas Eve get-together.

We didn't know what to expect, knowing that the married children could really have used an extra fifty dollars at that time of the year and that our two children at home were always needing money for gas and other things. However, we left the decision entirely in their hands.

When Christmas Eve came and the stories were shared, we were touched by the results. As each one told his or her experience of giving, tears flowed. All of us felt a truly special spirit, a poignant reminder of the true meaning of Christmas and of our many blessings as a family.

Becky and Bruce and their four children purchased all the gloves and mittens they could buy for fifty dollars, packed lunches, and went downtown on Christmas Eve day. They walked the streets where the homeless generally congregate and offered their bit of warmth and Christmas cheer wherever they saw the need. Their gifts were received gratefully, and the impact of the experience on their children was great as they came to realize that these people really did not have a place of their own where they could sleep or eat or get warm on that Christmas Eve.

Melinda, Cory, and their two little girls selected an "angel" from the Salvation Army tree at the mall in Orem. It identified Margaret, an elderly woman who needed a bathrobe and some socks, a woman who would have no one with whom to share Christmas. Our granddaughters were excited to shop for her, and they told us about the pretty pink flowered robe and socks they picked out. They enjoyed trying to imagine Margaret's face when she received these gifts from someone who cared about her.

Brent and Holly chose to make the holidays a little more special for missionaries in the Utah South Mission who wouldn't be receiving gifts from home and family. They prepared a Christmas basket for a sister missionary and one for an elder, including socks, ties, and holiday treats. They delivered these to the mission home to be given to those special missionaries. (Brent probably remembered being in Australia and not receiving his Christmas package from home until March, as sometimes happens in the mission field.)

Natalie also adopted a Christmas "angel" and explained why she chose

Gabriel, age nine. She had tried to imagine how disappointed her nine-year-old nephew would be on Christmas morning to awake and find no gifts under the tree. She purchased pants, a shirt, shoes, underwear, and a few toys for Gabriel, wrapped them, and delivered them to the Salvation Army station at the Cottonwood Mall.

Brandon, our eighteen-year-old prospective missionary, told of buying copies of the Book of Mormon, some in English and some in Spanish, to which he attached notes bearing his personal testimony. He left the English ones on doorsteps of some of his friends who were either nonmembers or struggling at the moment with activity in the Church or testimonies of the gospel. He gave the Spanish copies to his friend who was leaving that week for a mission in Spain, to be distributed there.

As our children and grandchildren expressed gratitude for the opportunity to focus on the spirit of giving and on the life and example of our Savior—the Lord's gift to the world that first Christmas Eve—we cherished our blessings as members of the Church more than ever. It truly was a memorable Christmas season for our family.

A Christmas Gift of the Gospel

ELDER GARY J. COLEMAN

As I look back on two particular Christmas seasons of many years ago, I realize that sharing the gospel with others is the most priceless gift we can give.

One of these memorable seasons began in the fall of 1975, when our family moved into a new home. My feelings prior to the move had convinced me that we would find a home near a nonmember family who were ready for the gospel. A few weeks after we moved into our home, my wife and I visited six of our neighbors on a fast Sunday afternoon. A family of six lived only two houses from us and we began to get acquainted with them. Within a few weeks they attended a ward Halloween party with us. Soon they were sending their children to Primary with our children. Next, the husband was playing basketball with me on Saturday mornings at 6:00 A.M. His wife began attending Relief Society with my wife. A Book of Mormon was placed in their home. Then a family home evening was held, followed by a first discussion.

I drove the missionaries home after the first discussion. When I returned to our neighbor's home to pick up my wife, the husband took me aside and said, "Can I ask you a question? Would you baptize my family and me on New Year's Eve?" What an exciting Christmas season for our two families as we prepared for this wonderful event!

A few days following their baptism, our neighbors were notified that they were being transferred to another city. How fortunate we had been to find and fellowship this great family within this crucial period! The Lord did most of the preparation. I know this work is his work. He prepares the way if we will but walk through the door opened by faith.

The other season I remember clearly was in 1962. As Christmas drew near, it was evident that unless my brother Jerry and I worked during the holiday vacation, we would not be able to continue college the following semester. So we both decided to work an extra week and go home toward the end of the vacation. I invited Jerry to share my apartment, since his dorm was closing and my roommates were going home. As we made our plans, I kept hoping an opportunity would arise for me to share the gospel with him.

A few weeks earlier, two days after my baptism into The Church of Jesus Christ of Latter-day Saints, I had seen Jerry near the campus. All of my family had had misgivings about my taking this step.

"Did you go through with it?" he asked.

"Yes," I replied. "I feel good about what I have done."

He looked into my eyes and surprised me with his next remark. "You're my oldest brother. I know you wouldn't have done it if you hadn't thought it was right."

A feeling of relief swept over me. *He hasn't cut me off,* I thought. *He still has respect for me.*

During the months I investigated the gospel, I had wrestled with the question, "Which church is true?" And, as the oldest son in our close family, I was especially aware of the role I played in leading my younger brothers and sisters. I had to be sure, absolutely sure, that I was doing the right thing. The hours, the days, and the months of turmoil as I sought an answer are still vivid in my memory. Finally, the answer had come one winter morning in the sweet, peaceful manner in which the Lord gives it.

Christmas vacation with Jerry turned out to be one of the most satisfying experiences of my life; it was a time of giving and sharing that I shall never forget. We spent almost every waking hour at the little kitchen table discussing the gospel. Our meals were almost incidental compared to our spiritual feasting.

Later, when we returned home to our family, I experienced a new appreciation for each member and sensed an acute awareness of my responsibility to share the gospel with them.

Jerry was baptized in March. What a glorious day! Now I had another member of the family who felt as I did about the gospel! We rejoiced together and discussed our hopes and concerns for our brothers and sisters. Our bond has grown stronger over the years, and we have since had the opportunity to widen the circle of family gospel involvement by baptizing our sister and her husband and by doing temple work for our kindred dead.

When happy Christmas memories come to my mind, prominent among them are those two special experiences when I had the opportunity to see people embrace the gift of the gospel.

Portions of this chapter are adapted from "Scriptures and Scrambled Eggs, *Ensign,* December 1974. © The Church of Jesus Christ of Latter-day Saints. Used by permission.

A Christmas Gift of Freedom

ELDER MONTE J. BROUGH

Often our most important experiences are somewhat challenging; we would not necessarily desire to repeat them. One of my most important lessons in life came to me as part of the Christmas season more than forty years ago. This Christmas experience, which is the one from my childhood that I remember best, occurred when I was twelve years of age.

I had been ordained a deacon on the twenty-fourth of June, a few days after my twelfth birthday. Being ordained a deacon was a great thrill to me, and I found this to be an exciting new event in my life.

I had a job delivering the *Deseret News* and the Salt Lake *Tribune* in my little hometown of Randolph, Utah. Randolph, a small town near the edge of Wyoming in the northeastern part of Utah, is in a valley at a high elevation, which results in severe weather conditions much of the time. Day after day, in summer or winter, it was my responsibility to deliver to the homes of the residents of our little community a fresh, new copy of the daily newspaper. I had a little pinto horse who carried me those many miles for several years in that important era of my life.

We could not afford a saddle for the horse, and so I rode her bareback. Although the ride was a little insecure, it was more comfortable during the cold days to sit on the warm back of our horse as we galloped around the town each day. My practice was to put the newspapers in two big sacks, with straps across my waist, slinging one sack of newspapers on each side of the horse to provide a good balance during the day's delivery. I was careful never to throw two in a row out of the same sack because then the sacks might become unbalanced and I would have a hard time staying on the horse's back.

On Sunday, July eighth, I was hurrying to deliver my newspapers on time so that I would be able to attend my priesthood meeting. It would be only my second opportunity since my ordination two weeks previously, and I very much wanted to be part of the meeting. With the large load of newspapers and my little horse traveling at full speed, I was an accident on the way to happen. My horse's feet became entangled in some net wire fencing; she was thrown hard to the ground along with me and all my newspapers. The force of the fall knocked me unconscious.

I did not recover consciousness until about eighteen hours later in a hospital in Evanston, Wyoming. There we learned that I had sustained no serious injuries except for a badly broken leg. The fracture was severe enough that the doctors in Wyoming felt I should be transferred to the Primary Children's Hospital in Salt Lake City. There my leg was set in a large cast and I was placed on crutches for the rest of the summer.

In September of that year, 1951, I began my first year of junior high school. Because the old high school had burned down some years previously, school classes were held in a variety of community locations, including the basement of the Rich County Courthouse. On the very first day of school, as I was trying to negotiate my way on crutches down a flight of concrete stairs into that basement, I tripped and fell, breaking my leg again.

The break was again considered bad enough that I was required to go to doctors in Ogden and Salt Lake City. They were afraid that if I had another accident the break would never heal properly, so I was required to spend nearly four months in bed or in a wheelchair. It was a confining, challenging time to have lost the ability to walk and the freedom of movement I had always taken for granted. I missed school, friends, my priesthood quorum, and my job as a newspaper boy.

This story still leads to a Christmas story. On Christmas Eve the casts were removed from my legs for the first time in five and a half months. I was given approval by the doctors to walk in a limited fashion for the first time on Christmas Day 1951. I shall never forget the exhilaration and freedom of being able to travel without the wheelchair or crutches upon which I had been most dependent.

It is interesting what the loss of a specific freedom does to enhance one's appreciation of other freedoms. I don't recall what material gifts I received that Christmas so many years ago; but I remember, as clearly as though it were yesterday, the tremendous gift of freedom that came with my restored personal mobility. I declared that I would never again take for granted the freedom to walk and run. I believe I have kept that goal. It was the finest Christmas of my life because of the precious gift of recovery that was given to me on that Christmas Day.

The Help of the Lord

E L D E R   J   B A L L A R D   W A S H B U R N

The memorable Christmas of 1952 found us living in a small, two-room apartment in Provo, Utah. Our first child, Mark, was four months old. Our twins, Jay and Kay, were to be born seven months later. We managed to find room for a Christmas tree in our crowded apartment. I had applied to several medical schools and we were anxiously hoping to receive word that I had been accepted.

On December 17 a letter came stating that I had been accepted to the University of Utah Medical School. We thanked the Lord, for we knew that without his help I would not have made it into medical school. We placed the letter at the top of the Christmas tree, where it remained during the holiday season.

When I was a senior in high school in Blanding, Utah, the superintendent of the school district, Zenos Black, decided to teach a class in math and chemistry that had not been taught before. This class proved to be invaluable to me.

Before my mission, I spent a year at Brigham Young University, majoring in music. Upon returning from my mission to the New England States, where I served under S. Dilworth Young, I re-entered BYU. The courses I liked best led me into medicine.

One of the most difficult classes required for entrance into medical school was organic chemistry. Without the math and chemistry class I had taken in high school, I would never have been able to compete with students from larger high schools who had studied chemistry for several years. The Lord had blessed me in high school and now blessed me again to make good grades in organic chemistry.

A few months after returning from my mission, I began dating Barbara Harries, from Columbus, Ohio, who was a senior in home economics education. We were married a few months later in the Salt Lake Temple. When we married, I still had eight more years of schooling and medical training ahead. We decided that we would not postpone having our family and that my wife would remain at home with our children. During those eight years of school and medical training, five of our ten children were born. It was a next-to-impossible dream to do what we did, but the Lord helped us to achieve our goals. This made it possible for us later to work for thirty years among the Indian people in Arizona. We were able to serve them both medically and spiritually, and this brought us great happiness.

We always had callings in the Church and tried to put the Lord's work first. He heard our prayers and answered them.

I would say to young people in the Church today, some of your happiest years will be the years when you are struggling to get through school and to get started in life. As long as you have each other and a love for the Savior, and are trying to follow him, you will be happy. You will have problems and trials, but they will help you to grow into what he wants you to become.

Among my treasured memories of Christmases past is a little Christmas tree with an acceptance letter hanging from the very top—a letter that represented our Savior's love for us.

The Boy Who Sang

ELDER F. MELVIN HAMMOND

Traditionally at Christmastime I have penned a poem, a story, or music and lyrics to a song as a gift of love for my children and grandchildren. My desire has been to strengthen their faith and appreciation of the gospel and to testify of the Savior Jesus Christ. The story that follows, which I wrote in 1992, is an example of this tradition. I had been studying the life of an ancestor who lived in Switzerland prior to the restoration of the gospel. One night I dreamed of a Swiss boy, which dream inspired this story.

There was once a boy who sang a great deal. He sang when he bathed. He sang when he herded the cattle. He sang when the sun went down beyond the wooded hill. He even sang in bed just before sleep closed his eyes.

All the villagers talked about the boy who sang. They said, "He sings very well, like a lark. One day he will sing on the big stage in the city and bring fame to our tiny village. We must present him to the Music Master."

The Music Master knew everything about singing. He listened to the boy sing. "You sing like a lark," he said to the boy. "But every song you sing sounds just the same. The tune is the same. The feelings are the same. You sing like a boy. Come to me again when you have something else to sing."

The boy became a fine, young man. Strong and brave he went to war. He went to fight for freedom. He went to save the village from the enemy. Many died in the battles. At night the boy sang. Every soldier heard his songs. He sang of peace. He sang of home. He sang of courage. He sang over the graves. The soldiers said, "Listen to him sing. Someday he will sing on the big stage in the city."

The war ended. The village was saved. Peace returned to the land. The boy who sang a great deal had become a man. The man stood before the Music Master, as he had done once before.

"Well," said the Music Master, "have you something different to sing for me?"

"Yes," the man replied. And from his mouth, bold and grand, came this song:

I am a warrior,
A warrior's man.
Mighty and proud
I stand.

The Music Master listened, frowned, and said, "Indeed, you are a warrior's man. But there is something missing when you sing. Come again when you have more to bring."

In the village lived a lovely girl. Her hair was shiny gold. Her eyes were the lightest blue. She heard the man sing. He sang to her with words of love.

Beautiful girl
So sweet and true.
I love you!
I love you!

And he did! She gave her heart and soul to him. They were married in the little church in the village.

Again the Music Master listened to the man sing. "Yes," he said, "You have changed. There is something sweet and lovely in your song, a certain brightness not there before. Still, you are not quite ready. I will hear you again someday."

In the happy spring the beautiful girl, now the man's wife, said, "When winter comes and snow has fallen you will be a new father." He laughed with joy.

On Christmas day the child was born: a little girl, tender and pale. She could not breathe. They tried to help, but failed. The very day she came to earth, she sighed and died.

The father buried her in a little grave. He knelt beside the spot. He put his hand on the tiny mound. The snow fell all around. He cried in sorrow for the angel child. And he sang this tender song:

My baby, my baby
Gone since birth.
Why couldn't you linger
Awhile on earth?

That night he sat alone, grieving for the babe. He closed his tired eyes and slept. He dreamed that he saw her tiny frame in heaven above. He saw his mother, who had left this life long ago, holding the baby girl in her loving arms. She smiled as she patted the little one, so recently come from him.

Suddenly there appeared one more glorious than the rest, who bent down and kissed the head of the dear, little child. Immediately the man knew that it was the Savior, Jesus Christ, who loved her too.

Everyone gathered around to welcome the baby to heaven. All the host turned their eyes on the grieving father. And it seemed as if they said, "Your angel daughter is not dead. She waits to see you here."

He awoke! His eyes were wet with tears. Yet his heart was filled with hope to know that she waited there for him. And he sang this song:

I thank thee, O Father,
For allowing me to see,
The meaning of
Eternity.

The boy who had become a man, a warrior, a husband, and a father stood before the Music Master. "What do you bring to me now?" he asked. The man opened his mouth and began to sing. The depth and goodness of his life rushed out in glorious sounds of music. The words were clear and the tones were rich and beautiful to hear. Everyone who was there cried because of such beauty—even the Music Master. He said to the man, "You came to me as a boy, a warrior, a husband, a father, but now you sing like an angel who has seen God."

Humbly the man replied, "I have!"

"Then you are ready," said the Music Master.

So the man sang on the big stage in the city. Fame and honor were brought to the little village. And all the people who listened to him sing said, "Today, we have heard the music of eternity."

"Silent Night, Holy Night"

ELDER JOSEPH B. WIRTHLIN

From time to time, if we are living worthily, the Spirit of God touches our hearts and minds in such a way that our lives are improved forever. A warm feeling penetrates our hearts. The still, small voice speaks to us quietly, communicating through a burning in our bosom. (See D&C 9:8.) Knowledge given to us from God draws us closer to him, sanctifying us and strengthening our desire to return to his presence.

During such unforgettable moments, revelation comes to us and forever alters our view, sharpening our focus on what matters most in life. We sense more profoundly our eternal relationship with God as the literal Father of our spirits. We also feel more acutely our complete dependence upon the merciful atonement of his Son, Jesus Christ. I had just such a revealing experience.

It was Christmastime in the Bavarian Alps in 1937. I have always loved Christmas. There is a special spirit about it. The chill in the winter air is the perfect counterpoint to the warmth that should fill our hearts as we contemplate the message of salvation found in the birth, the

life, and the resurrection of our Lord and Savior.

I experienced that warmth while serving as a missionary for the Church just prior to the outbreak of World War II. As you might expect, the possibility of armed conflict was very intense in 1937. But as Christmas approached, our thoughts were drawn to the Savior. We rejoiced in the privilege of serving him during that sacred season in the famous city of Salzburg, Austria.

On Christmas Eve, Elder Staker Olson and I visited the village of Oberndorf, nestled securely in the beautiful Bavarian Alps. It was a crisp, clear winter night. We walked under a canopy of stars, across the smooth stillness of new-fallen snow to a humble little church where a familiar melody beckoned with its message of hope and peace. Inside, a choir was singing in German a carol that brought warmth to our hearts on that cold winter night. Though we were far from our homes and families, we were filled with our Heavenly Father's love and comforted by his Spirit as we listened to the calming strains of "Silent night! Holy night!"

Perhaps that Christmas Eve was like the night that more than a century earlier had inspired the assistant pastor in that quaint village to write the words to one of the most beloved hymns in all of Christendom. In 1818, Joseph Mohr was walking in the mountains above Oberndorf when he was overcome with the sublime beauty that surrounded him: the towering, majestic mountains; the brilliance of the stars in the sky; the shimmering glow of moonlight reflected on snow-covered hills and valleys; and the warm, welcoming lights of the village.

The setting provided inspiration for the new hymn Joseph Mohr was writing for Christmas services the next day. As he made his way homeward, words and phrases came together in his mind:

Silent night! Holy night!
All is calm, all is bright
Round yon virgin mother and Child.
Holy Infant, so tender and mild,
Sleep in heavenly peace;
Sleep in heavenly peace.

Silent night! Holy night!
Son of God, love's pure light
Radiant beams from thy holy face,
With the dawn of redeeming grace,
Jesus, Lord, at thy birth;
Jesus, Lord, at thy birth.
(Hymns, no. 204.)

Joseph Mohr took his words to Franz Gruber, the church organist. Because the church's organ was broken, Gruber composed music for the new hymn on his guitar. The tune came easily, and the next day "Silent Night" had its first performance in that unique little church. Sung by its creators to Gruber's guitar accompaniment, it probably sounded a little different from the full, rich, harmonious version we sing today. But the message was the same.

As we listened to the choir's harmony while standing in the very same church where the first rendition of this sacred song was sung, we were spiritually moved. We were filled with the true spirit of Christmas.

As we left Oberndorf and walked about fifteen miles to our humble lodgings in old Salzburg, we spoke of life more confidently. Our goals and aspirations were clear, and we were both focused as to our direction in life. Much of our conversation centered on our Lord and Savior, Jesus Christ. We felt closer to him that Christmas Eve. As we savored that sense of God's love for us, we also felt an outpouring of his love toward all mankind. Even with the threat of war hanging heavily over Austria and the rest of the world, for one night, at least, "all [was] calm, all [was] bright." It was, truly, a "holy night," a Christmas that we will never forget.

We determined that we would be even more diligent in our missionary efforts to proclaim Christ's gospel of repentance, and we resolved that, upon our return home, we would serve the Master all our lives through magnifying our assignments in the Church.

It was a time to reflect with humble hearts on the attributes of godliness as exemplified by the perfect life of the Savior. We had been studying the Book of

Mormon. As we walked, we spoke of what we could do to follow Alma's great admonition to the "church which was established in the valley of Gideon" (Alma 6:8):

"And now I would that ye should be humble, and be submissive and gentle; easy to be entreated; full of patience and long-suffering; being temperate in all things; being diligent in keeping the commandments of God at all times; asking for whatsoever things ye stand in need, both spiritual and temporal; always returning thanks unto God for whatsoever things ye do receive.

"And see that ye have faith, hope, and charity, and then ye will always abound in good works." (Alma 7:23-24.)

We desired with greater fervor than ever before to be strong, faithful men with valiant testimonies, men upon whom the Lord could rely. We wanted to "always abound in good works"; to be kind and loving toward others. As missionaries, we had learned to preach and teach the great Atonement, the resurrection, and the restoration of the gospel through the Prophet Joseph Smith.

Although we missed the company of cherished family and loved ones, we did not dwell on our absence from home. I expressed my goal to find a girl with qualities of character that stemmed from a deep and abiding spiritual foundation. We now knew that the virtues and attributes enumerated in Alma's admonition were the qualities we were looking for. My companion had a similar goal to be married for time and all eternity. I did find a companion who possessed all those qualities I had hoped for. Her name is Elisa Young Rogers. She has exceeded all of my dreams expressed on that sacred night.

Of course, it wasn't just the hymn that had such impact on us. It was the song's message of "the dawn of redeeming grace." To think that the Son of God would come into the world so humbly, live his life so perfectly, teach his gospel so completely, atone for our sins so graciously, and do it all so willingly!

I pray that our hearts and homes may resonate with this marvelous message of love, hope, and peace during the holiday season and forever. With the apostle John, I testify that "God so loved the world, that he gave his only begotten Son, that whosoever believeth in him should not perish, but have everlasting life." (John 3:16.)

Christmas Blessings

ELDER ROBERT E. WELLS

It was the afternoon of December twenty-fourth. All Church employees had been given the day off, but I had some business matters that I wanted to finish, so I was still in my office in the high-rise Church Office Building. Helen and the children were expecting me home for last-minute Christmas preparations before our traditional Christmas Eve dinner and family program.

I was hurrying to finish a long and complicated matter so I could go home when the phone rang. It was President Spencer W. Kimball, the president of the Quorum of the Twelve at that time. All he said was, "Robert, are you busy?"

I felt that he must need me for something so my answer was, "Not at all. What can I do for you?" We had developed a relationship over the years when he had stayed in our home in South America and I had traveled with him and translated for him down there. From time to time, now that I was living in Salt Lake City and working for the Church, he would ask me to drive him somewhere or accompany him to a conference. I was always flattered and happy to have the privilege of serving or helping this great man.

His response was as I expected: "Robert, thanks. Could you please meet me by my car?"

I answered, "Yes, of course." He hung up without another word, so I called Helen and explained that there would be a further delay in my arriving home. I hurried down to the parking level. President Kimball had already arrived and was waiting. We got into his car, and as we drove out he explained, "I have a distant relative with a small son in the Primary Children's Hospital and they have asked me to give the boy a blessing, but the father can't be there. Also I have heard of a child from South America who needs a blessing, too. So I thought of asking you to go with me. Is that all right?"

I assured him that it was perfectly all right and that it was both a privilege and an honor to be his junior companion anytime he could use me. After we gave the two blessings that he had mentioned, he suggested, "Robert, I think there must be some Lamanite children here in this hospital who would like a blessing on

93

Christmas Eve. Shall we go find them?" I was fascinated and delighted. I thought, *What a kind thing for this busy servant of Christ to think of doing.*

I found myself accompanying President Kimball from nurses' station to nurses' station in that large hospital where we would ask, "Are there any Indian children here? Are there any Latin American or South American children here? Are there any Lamanite children from the islands of the seas? We would like to visit each one and give them a blessing. May we do that, please?" President Kimball was so loving and kind and tender that no one turned him down. The Spirit was with him in a beautiful way.

So we went from room to room and from bed to bed giving blessings. I did the translating when the children spoke only Spanish or Portuguese. I couldn't help much with one young Navajo boy who spoke little English. But it was obvious that he wanted a blessing and that he appreciated the spirit that President Kimball reflected that Christmas Eve.

As we drove back to the Church Office Building several hours later, President Kimball mentioned that his family was waiting for him just as mine was waiting for me. Then he added, "But they will forgive us, I am sure. What better thing could we do than give the gift of blessings of the priesthood on Christmas Eve. Isn't that what the Savior would want us to do?"

I treasure in my memory and in my heart that interlude on a Christmas Eve when this great apostle who would shortly become the President of the Church took some valuable hours away from his dear wife and family so that he could minister to the children in a hospital because that was "what the Savior would want us to do."

Christmas Memories

ELDER JACK H GOASLIND

Christmas. *Christmas!* The mere mention of the word summons wonderful memories of the smells, sights, and sounds of what should be the happiest time of the year. Who can smell the rich, sweet fragrance of pine, for example, and not think of Christmas? Can we recall the memory-laden smells of cinnamon or cloves, our mothers' cookies baking, or even pungent wood smoke, and not be swept into thoughts so nostalgic and warm that we are at once transported to the Christmas of our fondest memory? Our homes, our workplaces, even the outside air fills with smells that are, unmistakably and forever, *Christmas.* And because these memories are often called back by our senses, Christmas experiences are especially susceptible to almost instant recall, triggered by a smell, sight, or sound.

Among my most cherished memories are Christmases of a simpler era: those of my youth and childhood. Snow would be piled high by the side of the roads and in our yards, and we boys would sled in our street until well after dark, fearing that at any moment our mothers would call us

home for dinner, and at the same time longing for the warmth and joy that awaited us there. My mother has always been a wonderful cook, but at Christmastime especially it seemed that her meals, along with everything else about the season, were more memorable.

The bustle of city life was far enough from our neighborhood that we saw the Christmas decorations "in town" only when our parents took us there to shop or, as we grew older, we ventured there by ourselves. But there was excitement and anticipation about every day that drew us nearer to Christmas.

I remember the smell of coal smoke from the furnaces and stoves that warmed some of the homes in our neighborhood, and I remember returning to the comfort of our own warm and cheery home, made even more alluring by the sight of Christmas lights strung on the house and over our tree. Also adding to my future memories was the wonderful smell of the Christmas treats my mother baked. Those smells were as welcome, pervasive, and nostalgic as the smell of last September's chili sauce wafting out of houses on our street and into the warm, late-summer afternoon air. They were the smells of *home*, as much a part of Christmas as any decoration, any present under the tree, or any group of carolers wandering through our neighborhood on a still and chilly night.

I remember shopping for simple presents with money saved from paper routes, chores, and odd jobs. These were difficult years, and although I had a certain anticipation and enthusiasm for the gifts Santa Claus would bring, I don't remember them being so much the focus of our life then as they seem to have become now. We kept Christmas in a simple and homey way that drew us near to one another. Oh, there was certainly giving, receiving, and much of the magical spell that seems to rivet the attention of any child in every age, but somehow it was gentler, less sophisticated, decidedly "low-tech," and above all less hectic.

And I remember always—always—the special emphasis our family gave at Christmastime to the birth of the Savior, Jesus Christ. Then, as now, it occupied a central theme in our home, and we knew this from our earliest years. Thinking back, I'm sure that was what brought much of the joy that came in our home at Christmas as well as throughout the year.

My father was the bishop of our ward for many of my growing-up years, and that always meant to him, quite literally, that there were many dear souls who needed looking after. Dad had a way of involving the youth of the ward, as well as our family, in the work of caring for and helping the widows, the elderly, the down-and-out, and everyone who

needed encouragement or looking after. Christmas, of course, was always a time when extra care was needed. It was as though my father, with my mother on many occasions, needed to make sure personally that everyone was warm and healthy, had sufficient to eat, and felt as though he or she belonged to the group. The care my parents gave others in those years—and especially at Christmas—has lingered as one of my most poignant memories.

Much of what sustains our Christmas traditions from year to year are those memories of Christmas past. In Charles Dickens's immortal *A Christmas Carol,* Ebenezer Scrooge, when forced by the Ghost of Christmas Past to look at his childhood memories (painful though some of them were!), began to warm to the spirit of Christmas and understand what it could mean in his life. Our own memories have a powerful influence on how we keep Christmas as adults, and how we impart the joy of the season to our children and grandchildren.

In my childhood home, Christmas Eve was especially memorable, because that was when our parents would gather us in the living room and together, often with extended family and close friends, we would share the evening and hear once more the wonderful story of the birth of Christ, found in the second chapter of Luke. It is a simple story, devoid of much literary flourish, but one that never fails to recall to my mind and heart the great miracle and blessing of that event that changed the world forever. This little babe, lying in a manger, so helpless and so unable to care for himself, would come to a power and glory so magnificent that he would care for all of us. His birth, his mortal mission, his death and resurrection are all the message of Christmas: *that he lives!* And what that has come to mean to each of us is so significant, so important, so marvelous, and so reassuring that each of us should indeed join with the heavenly host, saying, "Glory to God in the highest, and on earth peace, good will toward men!"

Everything we remember and think and do in this Christmas season should be rooted in the wonderful memory of Jesus Christ, and him crucified. It should be there to welcome us as we unite with our families. It should reflect in our countenances on Christmas morning. It should preoccupy our thoughts in every Christmas carol we sing and accompany us to every party we attend. It should be manifest in our wandering through the mall, and should permeate our homes as we trim the tree, bake our traditional treats, or plan our Christmas dinner.

On Christmas morning, my brothers and I always wanted to sneak down early to see if Santa had been there. But we knew that it was our parents' wish that we come to Christmas morning having washed and fully dressed ourselves. The anticipation was nearly unbearable! But it taught me an important lesson about having patience for the good things in life.

Today, our childhood memories have passed into history as calmly and as comfortably as the hymn "Silent Night." They rest there among others on the shelves of our memory, to be called back to consciousness whenever they are trig-gered by the sight, sound, or smells of Christmas.

My wife and I have tried throughout our married life to instill in our children the values we learned to appreciate and honor in our youth. We have carried on traditions, begun new ones, and shared in the joys and sorrows of family, friends, and loved ones. We have adopted the tradition of calling for my mother, now well advanced in years, and, beginning early on Christmas morning, visiting the home of each of our children, sharing with them the joy of the day. It is a day rich in memories as well: children's happy faces, cozy family times, and the smell of roasting turkey filling the houses. A few days before Christmas, we still gather the family together to read and reenact the story of Christ's birth. Our grandchildren dress in the garb of the day—made sweeter by their cherubic faces smiling through makeshift costumes of bathrobes, with turbans fashioned from remnants of cotton or gold lamé.

Sometimes we have enjoyed wonderful and well-planned traditional holidays together, and other times we have observed that the Christmases we loved best were those that merely "happened."

One thing is sure: we and our family, along with all of the Christian world—and much of the non-Christian world—will continue to observe and keep Christmas. We will share it with our children and our children's children and they, in turn, will share it with theirs. The message of Christmas—the birth of the Savior Jesus Christ—as it was prophesied through the centuries and then came to pass, will remain the same: "For unto us a child is born, unto us a son is given: and the government shall be upon his shoulder: and his name shall be called Wonderful, Counsellor, The mighty God, The everlasting Father, The Prince of Peace." (Isaiah 9:6.)

God bless you and your family as you gather together this year and always, to remember and retain this glorious Christmas message in your homes and families, your hearts, and your lives.

The Most Beautiful Christmas Tree

ELDER MERLIN R. LYBBERT

The most memorable Christmases are the ones which give emphasis to extending friendships, strengthening family ties, and developing faith in Him whose birth the Season commemorates.

One such Christmas I vividly recall was in Northern Canada, where my parents with our large family homesteaded during the great Depression years of the early thirties. Our small log house was built to overlook the Beaver River as it lazily wound its way back and forth cutting large, half-circle meadows in the valley below. Our closest neighbors were several miles distant. Roads were little more than trails cut through the tall trees and brush. Winters were long and very cold. A perpetual blanket of snow covered the ground, from early fall until late spring. Each snowfall added to its depth and beauty, but presented an increasing challenge in carrying on the necessary functions of daily living.

Transportation was simple: we walked, or for longer distances Irequois, our sturdy horse, pulled a toboggan comfortably fitted with a horsehide blanket and warmed with a few hot rocks.

Thick blankets of snow etched unending scenery and enhanced the silence, causing one to feel that human presence was an intrusion upon nature. Only the chatter of a red squirrel high in a spruce tree, the drumming of a grouse, or the yap of a fox would break the stillness.

On one such day near Christmas Dad took us to find a Christmas tree. We could choose from a forest of pines. Which one would we choose? As children we looked for a small, well-shaped spruce that would fit into our low-ceilinged log house. Dad had something else in mind, and his eyes were cast much higher in the forest. Finally he said, "I think this one will do."

We couldn't believe his words. We were standing beneath a giant in the forest, perhaps ninety to a hundred feet tall and nearly two feet in diameter at the base. How could we use such a huge pine for our Christmas tree? Dad went to work with a Swede saw and a razor-sharp two-bitted axe. He felled the huge tree into an opening so that its fall was cushioned by the deep snow. We followed him to the tip of the tree, where he cut off about three feet of it. The rest would be used for firewood in due time. He stood the treetop before us. We were at once amazed and pleased, for it was perfectly shaped and covered so completely with tightly formed pine cones that there appeared scarcely a place left to attach an ornament, nor did it need any. The only adornments we added later were a few strands of popcorn that Mother helped us string on thread.

It was the most beautiful Christmas tree I've ever seen. There were few presents that Christmas, but Dad and Mother gave us much more. They gave an experience in family togetherness that we would always remember. There was no television, nor even a radio, but we gathered about a wood-burning "puffing billy," and by the light of an Aladdin lamp, Mother read the sacred story of Christmas from the scriptures.

Sacrificing to Share

ELDER L. ALDIN PORTER

In the predawn hours of a very cold, crisp morning in December 1950, my bus passed through Havre, Montana. The driver informed the passengers that the temperature outside was twenty-four degrees below zero. I had been traveling all night. It was still dark, with no moon, but the sky was spectacular with a canopy of stars flooding the heavens.

Late that afternoon we arrived in Poplar, Montana, a small government Indian village. This was to be my first field of labor as a newly called, nineteen-year-old missionary. As I left the bus stop and walked to the lodge, the snow crunched loudly beneath my feet. I was filled with anticipation but had no concept of the adventure or the eternal lessons in store for me.

This would be my first Christmas away from home, my first Christmas among strangers. To suggest that home seemed very far away would understate my feelings.

Several families in Poplar had accepted the message of the restoration. Two of those families made a significant and

lasting impression on my life during that Christmas season.

That memorable time began on Christmas Eve when my missionary companion and I went to the small home of an elderly widow to celebrate the holiday with her and several members of her family. We sang Christmas carols and read the sacred account of the first Christmas as recorded in Luke, concluding our evening with a small supper that we were sure strained her meager budget. We were humbled by her generous hospitality, and even more by the small gift she presented to each of us.

Whenever I read of the widow giving all she had in the temple, I remember this wonderful Indian sister in Poplar, Montana. She was willing to share all she had with the missionaries. "For all they did cast in of their abundance; but she of her want did cast in all that she had, even all her living." (Mark 12:44.)

The next day, on Christmas, a couple with two children under ten years of age invited us to their home. The excitement of Christmas filled that little home, even though we could see that they had only one small gift for each of the children. We watched as each child opened that single gift. The parents invited us to have dinner with them, but when we got ready to sit down, the table was set for only four. I whispered to my companion that possibly they had not expected us to eat with them. He assured me that our invitation had included dinner.

My companion and I were seated, along with the mother and father. The children played with their Christmas gifts while we ate. The meal was simple but prepared and served lovingly and with great care. For the first time in my memory at a Christmas dinner, I did not ask for a second helping. When we finished eating, the mother cleared the table and washed the dishes. Only then did the children eat. We suddenly realized that the family had only enough eating utensils for four people. The children had waited patiently for us to finish eating and for the dishes to be washed so they could eat.

One very humble missionary

returned to his apartment that Christmas night. At no other time in my life could I remember people being generous to me when they did not have ample resources to do it. These Saints of a different race had given to the missionaries the best they had when they had so little. They did not know me, but clearly they were honoring their Savior by honoring his servants.

"And whoso receiveth you, there I will be also, for I will go before your face. I will be on your right hand and on your left, and my Spirit shall be in your hearts, and mine angels round about you, to bear you up.

"Whoso receiveth you receiveth me; and the same will feed you, and clothe you." (D&C 84:88-89.)

My commitment to be worthy of the sacrifices of the Latter-day Saints was really born on that Christmas Day long ago. My prayers that night had new meaning as I pled with the Lord to bless those who had given me so very much.

The Truth about Christmas

ELDER REX D. PINEGAR

It was soon to be Christmas. My twin brother and I had reached the age when we knew the "truth" about Christmas— there really was no Santa Claus. Whatever gifts there might be would be bought from my parents' own small income. Our family's humble circumstances had always provided little help for Santa Claus. Max and I had decided between us that we would ease Mother's concern about it and so confided in her our knowledge. She merely replied, "Well, is that so?"

Christmas Eve came. Our family decorated the tree, made candy and popcorn balls, and placed our homemade presents beneath the tree. Dad sent us boys to bed, indicating that we were to stay there until he called us in the morning. Still laughing and giggling from the fun and excitement, Max and I followed our older brother, Lynn, to bed. With some effort on our part and some added encouragement from our father, we finally quieted down. Sleep came at last.

It seemed I hadn't been asleep long when Max awakened me with the news that it was 7:15 A.M.—time to hurry to the living room. Our excitement and noisy efforts awakened our father. As we reached the kitchen door we heard his somewhat irritated voice saying it was only 2:45 A.M. (we had read the clock backwards) and we were to get right back into bed and wait as we had been told earlier!

We turned back toward the bedroom. It was then that we saw it! Even in the very dim light it was beautiful! We sat down in the dark and described to each other a most unexpected surprise—a Hiawatha Streamer bicycle! It somehow didn't matter that there was just one bicycle, that there was snow on the ground outside and no place to ride, or that we couldn't read which of the children the gift was for.

It seemed that we sat there for hours, counting each tick of the clock and anxiously awaiting the call of our father. Finally we heard Dad's heavy footsteps as he walked from the bedroom. He hardly needed to beckon us to come.

There it was—"TO THE TWINS FROM SANTA"—the most beautiful bicycle we had ever seen. It was cream-colored, decorated with a bright red stripe and shiny chrome fenders, and completely outfitted with headlight, tool compartment, fender rack, reflector, and spring seat. We could hardly believe it was ours! Soon my brothers and I were clearing a pathway in the snow (shoveling the driveway had never seemed so easy) and were riding the sleek new Streamer. We ignored our cold hands and toes. What a wonderful time we had!

In my excitement and almost total preoccupation with our wonderful Christmas gift, I had failed to notice that there were few other gifts beneath the tree for other members of the family. Christmas stockings contained an orange in the toe, a few nuts, and some hard candy. Hand-wrapped pieces of honey candy and homemade fudge completed Santa's treat.

That evening as we went to bed, Max and I talked about the day's event—the bicycle. We planned how we would use the bike. We would get a paper route. We would have transportation to work during the summer, and we would be able to ride to school during the winter. It could be put to so many uses! Then our wonderment returned. Where had the bicycle come from? We knew Mom and Dad couldn't afford to buy it. We were also aware of the wartime shortages. Who had made this prized gift possible?

It wasn't until several years later that we learned the beautiful, heartwarming truth. The sacrifice and concern of a loving mother, brother, and sister had made possible that unforgettable Christmas. Our brother had worked extra hours at a

creamery after school. Our mother had saved money from her early morning work at the cannery during the harvest months. They had worked extra hours and had sacrificed their time, their earnings, and their own Christmas gifts to provide a special Christmas for the young twins. The happiness of that Christmas was surpassed only by the discovery of their secret and their love and sacrifice for us. Here was the true spirit of Christmas—an older brother and sister lending unselfish support to parents, desiring to give anonymously that which they'd never had themselves, seeking no credit or praise for their act, expecting no reciprocation. This example of the love of children for parents and brothers I shall always cherish and value as a priceless gift.

The bicycle is gone, long ago worn out by two energetic boys. Its shininess faded through constant use and enjoyment. The years, however, have only increased the glow of true Christlike love between family members. This act of love, and others like it, created ties that have brought our family members to the aid and support of one another many times and under every circumstance.

How valuable are the truths of the gospel of Jesus Christ taught to us in our homes. They strengthen us, bring us everlasting joy and happiness, and, if lived, bind us together in an eternal family relationship.

Christmas Traditions in Mexico

ELDER HORACIO A. TENORIO

Christmas celebrations were always very special, never-to-be-forgotten times during my early years. There are beautiful traditions in my homeland, Mexico, that have been passed on for many years and that create an environment of love and friendship.

Christmastime in Mexico begins on December 16 and ends January 6. During this time people remember the birth of Jesus Christ with different activities and with great joy.

The stage for the celebration is set by the *Nacimiento* (the birth), a display of figures made of wood, ceramic, or adobe representing shepherds, angels, the wise men, and the manger where Christ was born. This is beautifully decorated with landscapes such as small rivers, waterfalls, and sets of lights.

During the first nine days, from the sixteenth up to the twenty-fourth, a celebration called "Posada" (inn or place to stay) takes place every night. The Posadas represent the journey of Joseph and Mary to Bethlehem to be taxed. Every night during this journey they had to ask for a place to stay, or "posada," in

some of the homes they found along the way. Through the Posada this pilgrimage is represented.

To celebrate the Posadas, several families—relatives, friends, or neighbors—organize themselves so that during the course of the nine days each home will have the opportunity to receive the pilgrims. In some cities, neighbors get together and close off all the traffic on their block at night. They decorate the street from one sidewalk to the other with beautiful colored lights. Each host prepares a party for the guests during the assigned evening; in this way everyone has the opportunity to entertain the travelers.

The presentation is performed in the following manner: Two groups are organized; one group stays inside the house and the other stands in the street. The second group represents the pilgrims who accompany Mary and Joseph during their travel. Mary and Joseph are represented by two colorful, handmade adobe figures placed on a board. Each one of the pilgrims holds a little candle or lantern, and they come to the door and begin singing, asking for permission to come inside. Beautiful verses like the following are sung:

Outside Group
In the name of heaven
I ask for a place to stay
Because my dear wife
Is not able to walk.

Inside Group
This is not an inn
Go away.
I must not open
Lest you be some rascal.

Outside Group
Do not be insensitive.
Please, be merciful
Because the God in Heaven
Will surely reward you.

Inside Group
You can go away
Do not disturb anymore
Because if I get upset
I will beat you with a stick.

Outside Group
We come exhausted from Nazareth.
I am a carpenter, my name is Joseph.
My wife's name is Mary.
She has been anointed from heaven
And will be the mother
Of the Divine Word.

Inside Group
I do not care who you are
Let me sleep, please.
Again I tell you that we will not let you in.
Are you Joseph? Is your wife Mary?
Please, come inside, pilgrims
I did not know you.

Outside Group
May God pay you
For your great charity
And may the heavens bring
Great joy and happiness to all of you.

Inside Group
Blessed be the house that
Provides shelter in this day
To the pure virgin
Beautiful Mary.

The two groups sing alternating verses, and when they finish the doors are opened and the pilgrims are welcomed in. Once inside they sing again, this time together:

Come in, holy pilgrims, pilgrims
Receive this mansion.
Although it is a humble dwelling
I give it to you from my heart.

Now the party begins, and everyone sings:

Put candies and caneloni
For the boys who are too voracious
Neither do I want silver nor gold
What I do want is to break the piñata.

With this song the hosts begin to give little baskets with candies and caramel nuts to all present, and then they go to the back patio to break the piñata. The breaking of the piñata is a very special tradition. The piñata is made of a clay pot covered by different colored papers to give it the form of, for instance, a star, a clown, or perhaps an animal such as a donkey or an elephant. The figure is filled with fruits such as sugar cane, oranges, tangerines, limes, peanuts, tamarinds, and haws. When it is completely filled, it is hung from a wire or rope in the middle of the patio. Then the children take turns hitting the piñata with a stick about the size of a baseball bat. Their eyes must be covered with a piece of cloth and everyone else shouts, pretending to give directions to the person. This goes on until somebody finally hits the piñata, breaking it and spilling the fruits all over the floor. The children then run and happily try to get some fruit for themselves.

After the breaking of the piñata, the people sing Christmas carols, eat some snacks, and drink the traditional *ponche,* a hot beverage made of fruits such as apple, tamarind, haw, sugar cane, and a flower called jamaica. Sometimes this is followed by a dance for the adults.

The last Posada is on December 24, finishing earlier than the others so that the participants can go to their own homes for a more intimate family Christmas dinner.

On Christmas Eve, the entire family meets together to have the traditional meal of turkey, called *guajolote* in Mexico, codfish, *romeritos* (a native vegetable whose boiled leaves are served with shrimp and seasoned with chili) and *mole* (made of peanuts, chocolate, almonds, sesame seeds, toasted tortillas, and three different types of chili, among other things). This meal includes traditional Spanish candies, such as *mazapan* (almond paste), nougats, and candied almonds. That night children should eat and go to bed early because Santa Claus has to bring their toys and they must not be awake. During my childhood I would wake up early in the morning to see what

happy surprises Santa Claus had brought me that year.

This is a time of great outpouring of love, brotherhood, and friendship among the people and more especially among the family. Asking for forgiveness and having good feelings and desires are also very important during this time.

On the evening of January 5 there is another get-together of family and close friends. On this special occasion people share the *Rosca de Reyes* (similar to a fruit cake but with the shape of a doughnut). This *Rosca* can be very large, according to the number of people present; sometimes it covers the whole table. It is served with hot chocolate. As they share this light but enjoyable dinner, people exchange good wishes for the new year. Another tradition is to hide one or more small ceramic figures in the dough when making the *Rosca.* The individual who gets the figure in his piece is supposed to have a party in his house the next month.

This *Rosca de Reyes* celebration commemorates the visit of the wise men from the Orient who went to see the newborn king, Jesus, in order to offer him their presents. On the morning of January 6, the children also receive some presents supposedly left by the holy men of the Orient. These are usually clothes or other useful items rather than toys.

The Tenorio family also enjoys some particular family traditions. On December 24 we have a special family home evening where we sing Christmas carols, read the scriptures (especially the story of Christ's birth), and reflect about this transcendent event for humankind. We share our testimonies and pray, expressing our gratitude for the coming of Christ to this earth and for the fact that he would come as a helpless child, after having been a king and God, in order to grow and develop so that he could experience the sufferings and sorrows that would enable us to obtain eternal salvation.

This is the most special evening of the entire year for us. We dress in our best, as if we were attending a sacrament meeting, because we feel we are inviting Jesus Christ to be with us. We indeed feel he is our guest of honor because we are celebrating the day of his birth. We always keep in mind that perhaps he might decide to personally visit us, accepting our invitation. In fact, I testify that there have been times when the Spirit of the Lord was truly present.

This is Christmas for us: a time of rejoicing, of celebrating, of sharing with family and friends, and most important a time of remembering the Savior Jesus Christ.

Likening Luke 2 to Our Lives

ELDER JAY E. JENSEN

"There was no room for them in the inn." (Luke 2:7.)

Is there room today for Jesus in the "inn" of our hearts? Is there room for his doctrines, his ordinances, his teachings, his example? The world with all its attractions crowds him out of our hearts. Even with all the warmth, love, and special feelings at Christmastime, the tinsel, the gifts, the parties, the sales, the commercialism often leave no room for the Lord. The simple words "no room for them"—and especially for Him, the Son of God—are the great indictment of our day.

"And there were in the same country shepherds . . . keeping watch . . . by night." (Luke 2:8.)

When Jesus comes again, I want to be like the shepherds, keeping watch, doing my duty, at my post.

"Ye shall find the babe . . . " (Luke 2:12.)

The shepherds found the babe wrapped in swaddling clothes, lying in a manger. Never again will anyone find Jesus as a baby or in a manger. He is Jehovah, the God of Israel, the Savior Jesus Christ, a God who is a glorified, exalted being with all knowledge, all wisdom, and all power. Satan would like to keep in people's minds that Jesus is still a helpless infant.

"Let us now go . . . and see this thing." (Luke 2:15.)

There is an urgency about the work. Let us now go and visit the sick, the needy, the poor. Let us now go to the temple. Let us now go to Sunday meetings each week. Let us now go visit our immediate and extended families. Let us do it *now!*

"They made known abroad the saying." (Luke 2:17.)

The shepherds were good Saints. They "opened their mouths" (see D&C 24:12). I suspect that they "made known abroad the saying" first to their immediate families, and then to their neighbors and associates. They may have been much like Alma and Ether, who could not be restrained from testifying because of the Spirit that was in them (see Alma 43:1; Ether 12:2).

"Mary kept all these things, and pondered them in her heart." (Luke 2:19.)

We too can keep these sayings and

ponder them in our hearts. We can also keep sayings in our journals and notes to facilitate our pondering them.

"The shepherds returned [to their fields], glorifying and praising God." (Luke 2:20.)

We too must return to our fields and our homes and our offices and our meetings, glorifying and praising. We need to work, but we must do it with a renewed focus and purpose. Sheep need tending now as they did then. Faithful shepherds will always be found at their posts, with Jesus at the center of their lives and hearts because they know and love him.

Gratitude from Jerusalem

ELDER ROBERT K. DELLENBACH

On the day of Christmas Eve 1993, my wife, Mary Jayne, and I were in Jerusalem on a private visit. Kent Brown, the director of the Brigham Young University Jerusalem Center, invited us to join him, his wife, Gayle, and his daughter, Shoshauna, to tour a few of the places where the Savior walked.

Late that afternoon we entered the Palace of Caiaphas, a high priest who "belonged to the Sadducee party and took an active part in the attack made upon our Lord." (LDS Bible Dictionary.)

We descended the long stone stairway down into the prison, which was void of sunlight and ventilation, and felt the foul air surrounding us. Our hands became clammy and the feelings of pain and death were ever present. How awful must have been the scene as the Savior was cast into such abasement!

Underneath the palace are the dungeons where the prisoners were held. The cells were hewn out of solid rock. Chiseled into the walls are looping holes where chains were threaded to hold a prisoner fast.

As we wandered from cell to cell and saw the chain holes in the rock walls, the Savior's atonement became somehow more vivid to me. I felt the rudeness of the mock trial, the harshness of the voices, the gloating of the accusers.

Brother Brown had brought some small hymnbooks with him. We stood in the damp dungeon and sang the hymn requested by Joseph Smith in the Carthage jail just before his martyrdom, "A Poor Wayfaring Man of Grief." As I reflected on the Savior and the Prophet Joseph Smith, tears came to my eyes, uncontrollable tears, tears of compassion, tears of love, tears of gratitude for their selfless acts. My feelings of gratitude for them were overwhelming.

Why, on Christmas Eve, the celebration of the Savior's birth, was I sensing his death? Perhaps it was this awful place. Then, the thought came to me, *What was his mission here on earth? Why was he born?* The perfect Savior had little need of the earthly experience. The Atonement was his goal. All else pales in significance when measured against the full weight of this selfless act of mercy.

There we were, alone in a dank, dark

prison. How alone the Savior must have felt. How awful the insults and the injustices he endured!

That feeling of being alone touched me deeply. He alone trod the winepress. He alone was the Perfect Lamb of the sacrifice. He alone could atone for the sins of an ungrateful and sinful world.

Christmas is a time to celebrate the Lord's entry into this world, not his departure, not his death. Yet being there in that empty prison I could not help but feel the most profound gratitude for him, my Savior. His act of unselfishness, his forbearance, and the dignity with which he "descended below them all" (D&C 122:8) impressed me in the most spiritual way. How I loved him! I sensed his pain—including his spiritual pains of compassion for our sins and our suffering.

The message in 1 Peter 2:21-24 helped me to understand more fully his act of mercy:

"Christ also suffered for us, leaving us an example, that ye should follow his steps:

"Who did no sin, neither was guile found in his mouth:

"Who, when he was reviled, reviled not again; when he suffered, he threatened not; but committed himself to him that judgeth righteously:

"Who his own self bare our sins in his own body on the tree, that we, being dead to sins, should live unto righteousness: by whose stripes ye were healed."

And then I was reminded of Amulek's testimony: "And behold, this is the whole meaning of the law, every whit pointing to that great and last sacrifice; and that great and last sacrifice will be the Son of God, yea, infinite and eternal." (Alma 34:14; see also verses 15-16.)

The purpose of the birth of the Savior was even more profound than ever before in my mind. I knew of his mission long before my visit to Jerusalem. But on that day, in that dark abyss, thoughts of his birth and his atonement filled me with a gratitude and love for him which I shall never forget.

All Kinds of Christmases

ELDER RULON G. CRAVEN

I cannot remember a Christmas season when I have missed the opportunity to reflect upon the life and ministry of our Savior, the Lord Jesus Christ. Throughout my life, circumstances have sometimes taken me away from home during this special time of year, but always I have been buoyed up with a deep love for my Heavenly Father, the restored gospel of Jesus Christ, and my family and friends. This love has carried me through those lonely Christmas times.

As a young man, I spent two Christmases on board a ship during World War II. One of those occasions was uneventful because the only thing on board to represent Christmas was the evening meal of turkey, dressed with all the trimmings. While my shipmates played cards to pass the time and block out the pangs of being away from their homes, I gained pleasure and spiritual comfort from reading the Book of Mormon, especially Third Nephi. I was grateful that my parents had raised me to appreciate and focus on the spiritual side of Christmas more than the commercial side.

My second Christmas as a sailor was spent in Tsingtao, China. Our ship had been at sea for many months, and during that time I had not had an opportunity to attend any kind of church service. I went ashore with some of my shipmates to explore Tsingtao. After walking the streets searching for a church, I became aware that the Catholic church was holding a special Christmas Eve Mass. I had a strong desire to attend some kind of religious service, and because LDS services were not available in that port, I decided to go to the Mass.

Another sailor and I asked our superior officer for permission to attend the Catholic services, and it was granted—with the provision that we sober up four other sailors to accompany us. The task of sobering up those sailors to be in a fit state to attend was not easy. The best method we knew to accomplish this task was to hold each individually under a cold shower. We were not too popular, but our determination to attend a church service far outweighed their cries of indignation and displeasure.

I found the Catholic Mass interesting, but was somewhat disappointed to find the church building so full of people that we were barely able to stand. However, I noted with interest that despite our being crushed in, we were well within the reach of those who were gathering donations. I was able to contrast this service with those typical of my home ward in Boise, Idaho. I reflected on past experiences attending church with my family, talking with my bishop and quorum leaders, and enjoying great youth activities. All these memories came flooding back to me and gave me inner peace on that particular Christmas.

Spending Christmas as a missionary in New Zealand added even more strength, love, and peace to my testimony of the gospel. I was assigned by my mission president to work among the Maoris. A great spirit of joy and happiness always accompanied the Maori Saints. They displayed a special reverence for our Heavenly Father and the Savior, Jesus Christ. Everyone was greeted in the traditional Maori way—the *Hongi*—touching noses as a greeting and an expression of endearment or affection. Large meals of pork, potatoes, puhaa, and fish replaced the traditional Christmas turkey and dressing. South of the equator, Christmas is the hottest time of the year. The Saints in New Zealand would often spend Christmas afternoon at the beach enjoying the cool sea breeze and playing games on the golden sands.

As the years trickled by and I had the joy of being a husband and spending Christmas with my sweetheart, Donna, I experienced a new dimension of love, peace, and enjoyment. Then, as children were born into our family, we were able to draw on traditions etched in our own childhood Christmas memories to help establish important traditions with our six children.

One Christmastime tradition our family adopted was to invite Church members and less-active families to our home for a Christmas family home evening. We would have a special lesson on the life of the Savior and share our testimonies.

Another family tradition that brought us much joy was taking Christmas goodies and homemade craft items to neighbors and friends. This entailed more than just giving a Christmas gift. Our whole family visited the homes of our friends, singing carols and sharing a brief message, with each child reciting a part.

Now, after all these years, I realize just how extraordinary my Christmas memories are. A different dimension has now been added. I can sit down quietly with my wife, Donna, on Christmas Eve and read about the birth of the Savior, just as we have done for over forty years, but now that we do not always have our children with us in our home, this is a whole new experience. We rejoice in knowing that on Christmas Eve, wherever they may be, they are also reading the Christmas story from the scriptures with their children.

It doesn't really matter if it is a chilly Christmas Eve in America or a hot December night in the South Pacific—on Christmas Eve, wherever I am, I have a burning love for and a testimony of our Savior, Jesus Christ. I know he lives, and because of this knowledge and all he has done for me, I gain a greater appreciation of Christmas every year.

Some Christmas Thoughts

ELDER JOE J. CHRISTENSEN

God Bless You, Amy

Years ago, when our oldest child, Amy, was about eleven, I was asked to share a family Christmas experience that was meaningful to me. I wrote the following:

She stood there, her lovely face and eyes aglow as she mentally pictured a multitude of rich and joyous Christmas experiences. She had been challenged to select the one most memorable in her eleven short years.

She might have thought of traditional Christmas candlelight dinners, decorations for the tree and house, family caroling parties, the long-awaited dolls, practical clothes, beloved books, the bicycle she almost gave up hoping for, and on and on.

Then it came! "Daddy, the one I remember more than any other and enjoyed the most is the time we took the box of Christmas gifts to that other family. . . . " In minute detail she recounted our family's planning of a simple, though not original, idea to assist a family in which accident had handi-

capped the father and the family economy—details like wrapping each family member's gift, selecting the fruit and sweets, leaving the box on the porch, ringing the bell, running through the snow, and seeking protection in the shadows just long enough to see the children find the box. She even remembered how difficult it was for Susan and her to keep Stephen and Linda quiet so the family would never solve the mystery of where the box had come from. Of all her experiences, she remembered this the most vividly.

Simple? Yes. Yet to me this was amazing and enlightening. Old sayings and scripture that I had heard since Primary days took on new dimensions:

"It is more blessed to give than to receive." (Acts 20:35.)

"When ye are in the service of your fellow beings ye are only in the service of your God." (Mosiah 2:17.)

"Inasmuch as ye have done it unto one of the least of these my brethren, ye have done it unto me." (Matthew 25:40.)

Yes, the project was simple and not original, but somehow the approaching

Christmas season seemed to have a new warmth, charm, and meaning for me. God bless you, Amy!

A December Experience That Changed My Life

During the 1970s we had six children at home and life seemed very busy to Barbara and me. My work assignment at the time was to serve in the Commissioner's Office of the Church Educational System, responsible for the Seminaries and Institutes of Religion. At that time the weekday religious educational programs were being internationalized, and the work required a lot of travel outside the country.

It was the first week of December. I had just returned from a three-week trip into the South Pacific and, frankly, I was tired. Christmas was upon us and the schedule was full. There was much to do to catch up at home with the family, in the office, and in Church callings. I felt a little guilty because I found myself almost resenting December and all that was going on.

For some reason (and for me very uncharacteristically), I awakened at about 3:00 A.M. and lay there looking at the ceiling and thinking about all there was to do. I got out of bed and went into the study and began to write a few thoughts——thoughts that at the time really helped me. Gratefully, I lost every

feeling of resentment for the busyness of the season.

That was almost twenty years ago, and still, about the first day of December, I find renewed help rereading the words and then enjoying the season to the fullest—regardless of the schedule:

December is such a hectic time! There is so much to do.

There are Church, family, friends, work, school, community, concerts, dinners, weddings, shopping, programs, gifts, Scouts, cards, letters, cleaning, cooking, visiting, budgets, taxes, schedules, bills, snow, travel, noise, obligations . . . obligations!

But the day will come, sooner than we think, when family is gone, friends pass on, work ends, school is through, invitations thin out, pressures ease. One day there will be no children home to buy for, to clean and cook and sew for, no missionary out to pray for. Many obligations will end.

Thanks, Father, in the March, June, and September of our lives, for Decembers as hectic as these. May today's fevered stockpiling of memories help warm the Decembers of our lives.

Portions of this chapter were adapted from "God Bless You, Amy," *Improvement Era*, December 1964.
© The Church of Jesus Christ of Latter-day Saints. Used by permission.

The Gift of Life

ELDER MALCOLM S. JEPPSEN

As a child, when I got together with my friends in the days after Christmas, the question was always the same: "What did you get for Christmas?" Then we'd try to impress each other with a list of things we had received. Receiving gifts seemed to be what Christmas was about.

In my preteen years, I was told that the true spirit of giving was really the spirit of Christmas. Not receiving, but giving. I didn't believe it. I knew very well the true spirit of Christmas was getting.

As Marian and I watched our children during their process of growing up, we observed the same thing. We noticed that whenever a gift was placed under the Christmas tree, our children scampered to see whose name was on it. Then they seemed to want to get the presents all in a neat pile so that they knew what was theirs. Each was trying, I believe, to accumulate the most presents.

I wondered, as I suspect many others did also, if our families hadn't missed the true spirit of Christmas.

My father had the right idea about Christmas gifts. He gave the same gift to everyone, and that was stockings. When "one size fits all" came into vogue, his Christmas shopping became a breeze.

Eventually all of us grow up. We all do learn sooner or later that giving is really where the enjoyment of Christmas is. Even as a youngster I learned that Christmas gifts were fleeting. Trains did nothing but run around the circle . . . and eventually that was boring. Even back in my day our toys had batteries that would quickly run down.

But I received a Christmas gift one year that has never run out. My mother gave me this special gift. Mother was seriously ill during my early years. I was too young to realize it. I have precious memories of her preparing me for the time when she would soon die. She told me that she was going to a special place—a beautiful place—where only special people would be allowed. She told me that if I didn't get treated well by the family after she was gone, she would return and take me to be with her. That suited me fine. (Later, as life came to mean more to me, I hoped that I was being treated well.)

She died a few days before Christmas the year I turned eight. Mother had promised that she would see me baptized, and she did. The next day she went into a coma, and three days later she passed away.

Christmas was subdued that year, but I still had a feeling of closeness to my mother. She had always been the one to see that I had presents under the tree. That year, although we exchanged presents, we didn't have a tree. Somehow, though, I felt that Mother had left me a special present.

I looked about the house. I looked in those places where she had previously stored presents. I didn't know exactly what I was looking for, but I had the distinct impression that Mother had left a gift for me somewhere.

As it turned out, she didn't leave me a tangible Christmas gift that year, but she gave me the most wonderful gift that I could ever receive from another mortal. It was only years later, while attending medical school, that I learned what that gift was. Her illness was caused, in large measure, by carrying me to full term in her pregnancy. She had given her life so that I could have mine. I then learned the meaning of the Savior's statement, "Greater love hath no man than this, that a man lay down his life for his friends." (John 15:13.)

How tenderly symbolic was this gift of my life from my mother. How much more has the gift given by our Heavenly Father of his Son to the world meant to me since that realization. For through His gift, we have life, and that eternally.

Remembering

ELDER CREE-L KOFFORD

Across the East River, sheltered by a soft and inviting blanket of still-falling snow, lay magnificent Manhattan—my city. (Never mind that millions of others also call her their city. She's big enough and grand enough to accommodate all of us.) Her majestic towers seemed to reach the sky and beyond, their crowns hidden among the thick clouds that bonded heaven to earth. The thousands of lights twinkling in the crisp night air resembled a miniature galaxy, and the array of steel, glass, and concrete created an endless fantasy of shapes and forms.

It was Christmas in Manhattan, and I was on my way to check on some of our missionaries who were laboring in the city. As I drove through the giant canyons created by man's ingenuity and skill, my heart raced as the city's vibrancy reached out and enfolded me. Central Park, clean in its new white coat, rested, waiting for another day. In the near distance loomed the Tavern on the Green, with its myriad Christmas lights. Turning down Fifth Avenue, I passed Rockefeller Center, an oasis of serenity in a city of otherwise endless movement. Its

fifty-foot Christmas tree reigned proudly over the skaters crowding the ice rink that lay at its feet.

I stopped and took in the grandeur of the scene. Something, perhaps the majesty of the tree, brought back a feeling of a Christmas long-since lived. As I pondered, I found myself remembering that Christmas, when the world was locked in war. I was nine or ten years old then and still anticipated Christmas with childlike eagerness.

My family lived on a farm. Money was in short supply and, due to the war, Santa had only a limited number of toys and other Christmas goodies. In an effort to supplement the income from the farm, my father undertook to cut Christmas trees and supply them to tree lots. All the necessary permits having been obtained, our whole family (all five of us) climbed in the front seat of "old Emily"—our 1936, one-ton, flatbed truck—and started out for what we called West Mountain.

For days on end, we chopped and sawed and hauled. When the work was finally completed, I remember my father turning to my mother and saying, "Now let's find us the prettiest tree we've ever had."

Within a short time, it had been spotted. As our family gathered around the tree, we each in turn exclaimed that no tree that had ever lived had been so beautiful! It would later serve as the center of our family's Christmas festivities. The glow of the warm coal stove, the smell of freshly baked Christmas pies, and the wooden toy gun brought by Santa will always remain in my memory.

Thank you, Rockefeller Center, I found myself thinking, *for reminding me of such a beautiful moment.*

I drove on down Fifth Avenue and finally came to Lord and Taylor's, one of the city's giant department stores, where each year the windows were beautifully decorated with different Christmas scenes. It was not the scenes in the window that caught my eye, but rather a little girl with long, blonde hair, whose nose was pressed up against the windowpane. With a gleeful expression, such as only little girls can have, she excitedly watched the miniature figures move on their mechanized courses.

There, in the midst of this busy, bustling crowd, I had a moment of peace settle over me and a memory haunt me that I could not define. It was several seconds before I finally realized what it was. In reality, it was a memory I had never experienced, except vicariously. It was a picture I had seen only through the eyes of others, as they had told and retold it until it seemed to be my own story. Now my wife of nearly forty years, the little girl in my memory was skinny, with big, round green eyes and nearly white

pigtails. She would look forward with eagerness to each coming Christmas in Kanab, Utah—which was "her town."

Her favorite store was the Equitable, where an endless supply of things to delight young people always seemed to exist. On the mezzanine floor were all the shiny bikes, sturdy wagons, and cuddly dolls that any young girl could ever hope to see. There, in my mind's eye, was Ila with her face pressed up against the windowpane, eagerly anticipating the joys of Christmas. My heart melted as I thought how lucky I had been to find her and to claim her as my own.

I didn't even know who the girl at the Lord and Taylor window was. But for just a moment she seemed like my Ila, and I will always be indebted to her for allowing me to relive that vicariously created memory.

My visit with some of the missionaries completed, I headed back uptown toward the Church visitor's center, across from the Lincoln Center. Small, white clouds were rising from holes in the streets, as the moisture from the underground city of Manhattan rose into the night air, creating a fantasy of color and movement.

On the corner where I expected to meet my next missionaries, a large crowd was gathered, encircling a very grateful street vendor, whose inventory of smoked pretzels, hot nuts, and other assorted goodies was rapidly being depleted. Steam rose from the hot-water compartment of his "store-on-wheels" and sent a festive message to all who saw it. People reached their hands out eagerly to be warmed at the vendor's cart and then, having made their purchases, they hurried on.

As if by Santa's magic, I was transported back to a time in my childhood when our entire Mutual organization of ten or so young people gathered around a large, potbellied stove, its sides turning a dull red as the heat became more intense. The warmth felt good in the old building we used for basketball on weekdays, Mutual on Wednesdays, and Sunday School, priesthood, and sacrament meetings on Sundays.

Our Mutual leaders had settled on this as a fitting finale to our earlier activity of skating across the "sinks" east of town. On top of the stove was a large metal pot filled with hot chocolate.

Why would I remember that moment? Hot chocolate is not unique. There have been dozens of stoves like that one in my life and many, many Church activities. Even more interestingly, why would I think of a small, rural farm community while standing at one of the busiest intersections in the world?

Perhaps it had to do with the warmth of friendship, which I associated with that evening. Perhaps it was because, in my mind's eye, I saw old friends from grammar school days with whom I did everything that young boys living in the country would do. Perhaps it was the genuine feeling of love that came from the leaders. I found myself saying, "You know, they really did care."

I was roused from my reverie by the voices of a pair of now tardy missionaries, yelling across the street, "President Kofford!" We talked and parted.

As I drove away from my city, I couldn't get the faces of the missionaries I had seen that night off my mind. For all the memories that this evening had resurrected, it had created a new one that I would find returning, year after year, bringing with it the same warmth and fullness as those other memories of so long ago.

You see, many of the missionaries, on this particular year, had decided that they didn't want to have anything for themselves. A substantial number of them, using the missionary grapevine—one of the most effective communication systems ever devised—had agreed that whatever money or gifts they received from home would be shared with others.

As I drove north through Harlem and ultimately through the Bronx on my way out of the city, I passed by small apartments—some, little more than basement shelters—where the missionaries changed lives with the greatness of the gospel message. I found tears streaking my face.

That year our missionaries came to a fuller appreciation of just what it means to have Christlike love and how it feels to give selflessly to others. I'm not sure how many parents ever really knew that the beautiful gloves, the sweaters, the scarves, the candy, and all those other things they sent to their missionaries really ended up under the trees of people their sons and daughters loved more than they loved themselves. Boys and girls who would otherwise have had to say, "I guess Santa couldn't find where I lived this year," were instead treated to a Christmas made possible by the love of many of the young men and women of our mission.

Today, every time I pass a missionary, every time I see a gift package from home going to a missionary, and every time I think of the Christ Child and his great gift to us, I relive in memory that year in the mission field when young people who had already given so much gave even more.

What Do You Mean, "No Room"?

ELDER GRAHAM W. DOXEY

The time had come for us to move back to the city, but we were not yet ready to sell our country home. Our four years there—sixteen wonderful seasons—had been packed with the aromas of fresh milk, alfalfa wet with new rain, burning logs, and hay in the barn. We had savoured the quietude, the distance between us and the rest of the busy world, which let us hear water peacefully murmuring in the canal, the milk cow grazing, the silence under the stars, the fingers of a breeze running down the keyboard of the dried corn stalks.

"Don't you dread the thoughts of winters in that high altitude?" a city friend asked. No, they are wonderful: a welcome relief from fighting the weeds of summer. What could be more beautiful than the flight of large snowflakes and the peace and wonder as you open the door after a heavy fall. Winter is glorious but, like many things in life, after a time the welcome grows thin. There comes a point when we look anxiously for green signs of the fresh new visitor: spring. Summer and fall each have their own glories. Our few years of feasting on these were not enough. We were not ready to cut our tethers to the country time of our lives.

The perfect solution was found when our married children wanted to have their turns in our log house in the country. Christmas traditionally brought the large and scattered family together, and for weeks my wife and four unmarried daughters and I looked forward with great anticipation to returning to the cosy house for this special family time. Although we were the parents and had always been the 'hosts' at these affairs, this year we were to be guests. As we prepared for the event, planning food and gifts and accommodations, we began to appreciate the difference between the roles of 'guest' and 'host.' It became apparent that this year was going to be pleasantly different. We didn't remember that as one gives up responsibility one simultaneously gives up some control.

The snow was beautiful the night we arrived. Fourteen inches had collected on the driveway. We cut a track to the garage, which was at the rear of the house and set some distance away. The car had been fully packed, but the children were anxious to get into the warmth we could almost feel. The beckoning glow of light flowed from the windows of this home we all loved. My wife and I were left with far too many bundles to carry in one trip. Yet, standing in snow nearly to our knees, and being dusted as we were with the new fall, we found yet another finger to hold a string and a place to tuck yet another parcel so as to avoid a second trudging of the distance between the car and the back door.

With every other part of my anatomy dedicated to balancing my load, I tapped gently but anxiously on the door with my foot, hoping that someone would be close and would quickly open it for us. No response. I tapped again, a little less gently. No response. I called out as I pounded the next time. Silence from inside the house. From inside me, growing disturbance. Then my wife said, "What does that note on the door say?" I looked up, dripping a bit from the snow on my head, to see the words, "No Room in the Inn." *Someone,* I thought, *is trying to be clever, but it is not appropriate now.* I pounded again and said in a loud and proprietary voice, "We have a heavy load and want to get into the house, now!" Silence. I asked where the children were who had just jumped out of the car, the ones who should have been carrying some of these things that were burdening me. We then realized that they hadn't gone through this door either; their tracks reversed and went back to the driveway and around the house to the front. That seemed ridiculous. I didn't want to do that. But my good wife had

already started back through the snow, and I followed.

There was no path, only deep snow that was packing around my ankles and legs. We "broke trail" around to the front door. Here was shelter from a covered porch, and a doorbell. We rang. No response. The lights were on, but no one came. Only another piece of paper: "No Room in the Inn!" I rang a second time and called out loudly that we were cold and tired and burdened, and that we had read the cute message, but now it was time for them to open the door for us. Silence. I lowered the volume of my voice, but said so my wife could hear, "Whose house is this, anyway? Don't we still have some rights here?"

An anger and warmth was developing inside me that began to eclipse the discomforts of my cold body. If we couldn't get in the back door or the front door, what did they expect us to do? I seriously considered getting back into the car and heading for the city. I was not in the mood for these childish games.

There was yet another entrance, a sliding door to the family room from the patio. Again, tracks showed that our carefree children had gone before us. The quietude I had previously known in this spot was forgotten as my impatience and anger rose. How could the ones inside be so thoughtless of us and our miserable plight? As I waded again in the deep snow I knew that this year's Christmas reunion was going to be a bust. Bah, humbug!

At last the sliding door opened, and we stumbled through. I kept my face down, struggling to control my emotions so that I could be civil. Gradually I became aware that our family room was quite different. I first noticed the smell of hay; looking up I saw that there were hay bales where the furniture had been. In the corner were some of our grandchildren dressed as Mary and Joseph and lambs, our own live nativity scene. A real manger was set up. We saw young Mary holding her new baby. The children were excited but reverent. The hosts were warm, but a little apprehensive about having so rearranged our home. They made apologies about the inconvenience. I began to cool off as I warmed up to this occasion.

This was the Christmas when I first began to appreciate Joseph and Mary. I had truly felt the frustration of "no room!" Since then, as a parent, I have found ever-enlarging lessons in the stories of Mary and Joseph. Like them, I too have felt to flee to another place so that the evil forces would not destroy my child. Like them, I too have worried as my young teen has been away from me. I try now to look beyond the moment and see the wonder, the potential, the nobility in each of these eternal sons and daughters. I try harder to recognize times when I should be making 'more room' for a Joseph who is full of real frustrations— times when I should be listening for, and opening up to receive, the Son of God.

Christmas: A Time of Hope

ELDER VAUGHN J. FEATHERSTONE

I was raised in a family of five boys and two girls; a sixth boy died from pneumonia. We were poor due to a problem my father had with alcohol. We had few comforts in our home—no refrigerator, only an old icebox. We would buy a block of ice and put it in the top of the icebox, and it would take two or three days to melt to nothing. Our furniture was old and used. Most of our clothes had been given to us. We had little money and sometimes little food.

Children love Christmas, and we were no exception. Christmas was an exciting time for us because we somehow had hope that we would receive gifts from Santa Claus. We hardly ever put our tree up until the day before Christmas. We would have liked to put it up and decorate it earlier, but Christmas trees were too expensive. We had to wait until tree-lot owners would sell their trees for practically nothing just to get rid of them.

One Christmas I made a gift for my mother at school. It was a cardboard cutout of a tramp with his back to the observer. He was dressed in old bib overalls and had a patch on the seat of his pants. The patch was made of sandpaper. Printed on his back were these words: "Scratch your match on my patch."

That Christmas, and every Christmas, my mother got hardly any presents except what the children made for her at school. I do not remember my father ever giving her or any of the children a gift. He may have, but I cannot recall it.

The clumsy little gift I made for my mother hung on the wall by the stove for at least ten years. She would have been a wealthy woman if she could have had a dollar for every match she struck on the patch. The other children also gave her gifts they made at school or Primary. A dollar would have paid for all the materials it required to make all the gifts, collectively, for our mom.

Mother had a way of making every one of us feel that the gifts we gave her were priceless. I can remember the true excitement and gratitude she showed when she opened her simply wrapped presents. Years later, as a parent, I understood the sincerity in her gratitude. It was not until our children were old enough to bring us Christmas gifts they had made at school and wrapped themselves that I knew—knew of the thrill of a child giving a gift he or she has personally created. Those were sweet and precious memories of our mother and Christmas.

One Christmas Eve afternoon about two o'clock, mother gave us children seventy-five cents to buy a Christmas tree. We walked three blocks to Eleventh East and Wilson Avenue where there was a Christmas tree lot. There were a few scraggly trees left. We selected one about six feet tall and asked the owner how much it was. Somehow when the bargaining ended we had a "magnificent" six-foot tree with character and a few branches on it, and the tree-lot owner had our seventy-five cents. We proudly carried the tree home. We thought it was beautiful. I can still smell the clean, fresh odor of the Douglas fir as we made a stand and stood the tree up against a large wall in the house.

We had decorations that we kept from one year to the next. One was a tall, churchlike spire that was made of glass but was silver in color. We always loved to see the top of the tree adorned with that beautiful decoration. We would string a strand or two of lights—that was always the oldest brother's task—and then all of us would put on the ornaments. I remember Christmas chains we had made out of poster paper at school, chains twelve and fifteen feet long that we would drape over the tree from one branch to another. Mother would make a big bowl of popcorn and string the popped corn together in a long strand, and this too was draped over the tree.

Our oldest brother somehow managed to get half a dozen boxes of "icicles," silver strands of foil that he carefully hung one by one from the branches. We thought no tree ever looked more beautiful. We thought Steve had some kind of special talent and a great deal of patience to hang each individual icicle. I would not begin to know how long it took us to decorate the tree.

During that time our mother, who always tried to make holidays special, began to bake cookies, cakes, bread, and other treats we could afford. Always we would clean the house early in the morning and get everything ready for our tree and Christmas and, hopefully, Santa Claus. That must have taken three or four hours, considering all the fooling around we did.

After the tree was decorated, we went to the window; there were no drapes, just some worn, thin curtains. We pressed up against the window and looked down the street. Every year Uncle Ernest, my mother's brother, would come. He would usually bring a turkey or a ham, a half box of oranges, nuts, and lots of other food. This was a man who somehow knew what Christmas meant to us and could not let us be disappointed.

I remember we were all watching out the window with great anticipation when he drove up. We exploded out of the house, ran to the car, jumped up on the old "running boards," and looked through the car window, scanning for Christmas packages that were there, as always. I imagine Uncle Ernest looked at our clumsy little tree with a few home-wrapped gifts for Mom and hardly anything else there. Of course, we were too young to really observe, but I can picture him eyeing the cupboards, nearly empty, and being greeted by our mother, his sister, in the kitchen with an ineffable glow of tears and gratitude for what he was doing. Uncle Ernest probably reviewed all these things and more as he returned home. Somewhere from deep inside this holy man (who was not a member of the Church) there must have come a sweet whisper, "Thank God I came."

Uncle Ernest lived in Stockton, Utah, about thirty-five miles southwest of Salt Lake City. It took him at least an hour to drive to our home. He would spend another hour with us and our mom, and then he would drive back home alone. I imagine during Christmas Eve day he must have been swamped with things he had to do. He had four daughters, a wife, and his widowed mother to think about. He must have considered all of the activities of the day and seen no way to fill all the demands on his time and his hard-earned money, wages he received from working underground at the Bauer Mines. He undoubtedly had to leave some things undone and unbought. I wonder if he will ever know what his annual pilgrimage to our home on Christmas Eve meant to seven poor, ragged children and a heavyhearted mother. Maybe he did know, and that is what kept him coming year after year.

I remember one Christmas after my older brother was married. I was working forty hours a week and going to high school. Everything I earned, except two dollars a week, I gave to my mother to

help support the family. Mom worked at Garfield Smelter in a "man's job." She dressed in heavy overalls and heavy work shoes. She generally worked the graveyard shift so she could be with the family during the day. It took all we could both make to pay the bills.

During December our high school a cappella choir would often sing at wards and other places. I did not have an overcoat and always wore the same sport jacket or none. That year we sang outdoors at the monument in the Sugarhouse Plaza. It was snowing lightly and the wind was blowing. It was bitter cold. Several of my friends said to me, "Where's your coat, aren't you cold?" I said, "No, I don't get cold," but I remember the embarrassment I felt. It seemed like every time we sang out somewhere I was asked where my coat was.

That year I decided to ask Mom for an overcoat for Christmas. It was all I asked for. Somehow I knew I would get it; after all, I gave her all I earned to help with the bills. Christmas Eve came and we stayed up late. Finally we went to bed, excited about what Christmas morning would bring.

We children got up around 5:00 A.M. and rushed into the living room; our mother stayed in bed. I ran to where my stocking was, fully expecting a coat. There was no overcoat, but some other gift from Santa. The disappointment I felt was exquisite. I remember thinking I deserved an overcoat; it was all I had asked for. I didn't want the coat for warmth, I wanted it to keep me from being embarrassed. I remember thinking, *Mom, I gave you all I earned except a little.*

Surely I deserved a coat. This feeling lasted only a moment, and then I grew about a yard taller. I looked around the room; most of my brothers and sisters were equally disappointed. One sister had asked for a watch, and of course she didn't get it. Soon I was going to each one saying, "It's all right. She did the best she could. We need to show her how happy we are for what she did get for us."

Then I knew why Mother had stayed in bed. She couldn't bear to see the disappointment in our faces. By the time she came in, everyone was happy and excited over Christmas morning. Then I knew that I did not want an overcoat. It would have been like a major transgression to have gotten one that year for Christmas.

One year the best gift I remember came from God. Early that Christmas morning it began to snow heavily. In about an hour it had snowed four or five inches and was still falling hard. We all dressed up warmly and went out into the most beautiful white Christmas morning you can imagine. We played and frolicked in the snow. To this day, that still remains the most beautiful Christmas morning I can remember.

Christmas is a time of great hope. It is a season for loving and sharing. There are such things as priceless gifts, gifts that cannot be bought with money. In the twenty-fifth chapter of Matthew the Savior refers to the blessings that come to those who understand these gifts. Those who live closest to this pattern of living feel they are the most distant from it. The truly humble will never believe they are humble. The truly Christlike will feel the least worthy. If someone asked my Uncle Ernest or my mother if they practiced charity, "the pure love of Christ," they would both be terribly embarrassed and suppose that they were least among the disciples of Christ.

My heart is filled with love as I wish you a Merry Christmas, a holy holiday, and a bundle of rich treasures of the gospel.

Some Little Lessons from Christmas

ELDER SPENCER J. CONDIE

The German people have added a great richness to the celebration of Christmas with their well-established tradition of the Christmas tree and the contribution of many beautiful Christmas carols, including "Away in a Manger," "Ihr Kinderlein Kommet," "Es Ist Ein Ros Entsprungen," and the greatest Christmas hymn of all, "Silent Night."

I had already experienced one Christmas in Germany, but the most memorable of all was the Christmas of 1961. World War II had ended sixteen years previously, and the German economy was described by many as an "economic miracle," a miracle made possible by the industry and thrift of the Germans. But their economic recovery as a nation was not yet complete. Very few people had telephones and even fewer had automobiles. It was against this background that we celebrated Christmas Eve with a German family that was large by European standards, consisting of four girls and a boy.

The mother had joined the Church several years previously along with her older children, but the father had consistently resisted baptism. He had a severe drinking problem. On many occasions he was very unkind to his wife and children, and though he was friendly to us, he continued to resist our invitations to receive the discussions and be baptized. As young missionaries, we had formed a stereotyped opinion of this man who generally smoked when we were in his home and who often had a bottle of beer by his side. We judged him to be a very inadequate father.

Then the miracle occurred. The spirit of Christmas began to pervade everyone's hearts and homes, and this struggling family invited us to celebrate Christmas Eve with them. As we arrived at their little apartment on Christmas Eve, we quickly observed that there was no smell of fresh cigarette smoke in the air and there were no beer bottles in sight. After we exchanged pleasantries, the family lit the candles on the Christmas tree and the father, assuming his patriarchal role, gathered his children around him, reached for the large family Bible, and began to read from chapter 2 of Luke:

"And it came to pass in those days, that there went out a decree from Caesar Augustus, that all the world should be taxed.

"(And this taxing was first made when Cyrenius was governor of Syria.)

"And all went to be taxed, every one into his own city.

"And Joseph also went up from Galilee, out of the city of Nazareth, into Judaea, unto the city of David, which is called Bethlehem; (because he was of the house and lineage of David:)

"To be taxed with Mary his espoused wife, being great with child.

"And so it was, that, while they were there, the days were accomplished that she should be delivered.

"And she brought forth her firstborn son, and wrapped him in swaddling clothes, and laid him in a manger; because there was no room for them in the inn.

"And there were in the same country shepherds abiding in the field, keeping watch over their flock by night.

"And, lo, the angel of the Lord came upon them, and the glory of the Lord shone round about them: and they were sore afraid.

"And the angel said unto them, Fear not: for, behold, I bring you good tidings of great joy, which shall be to all people.

"For unto you is born this day in the city of David a Saviour, which is Christ the Lord.

"And this shall be a sign unto you; Ye shall find the babe wrapped in swaddling clothes, lying in a manger.

"And suddenly there was with the angel a multitude of the heavenly host praising God, and saying,

"Glory to God in the highest, and on earth peace, good will toward men.

"And it came to pass, as the angels were gone away from them into heaven, the shepherds said one to another, Let us now go even unto Bethlehem, and see this thing which is come to pass, which the Lord hath made known unto us.

"And they came with haste, and found Mary, and Joseph, and the babe lying in a manger.

"And when they had seen it, they made known abroad the saying which was told them concerning this child.

"And all they that heard it wondered at those things which were told them by the shepherds.

"But Mary kept all these things, and pondered them in her heart.

"And the shepherds returned, glorifying and praising God for all the things that they had heard and seen, as it was told unto them." (Luke 2:1-20.)

The father gently closed the Bible, and each of us wiped tears from the corners of our eyes. Notwithstanding all his weaknesses, this young father had risen to the majesty of the moment, and as the patriarch of his home he had become the Lord's instrument in inviting the Christmas spirit, the Spirit of Christ, into that little home.

We then sang several songs with the family, and no one seemed to be in a hurry to open their gifts that Christmas Eve. We sang some of the Christmas carols two or three times, and we never seemed to tire of the spirit they brought into that home.

Eventually it was time to open the gifts, and it became apparent that this man who was struggling to make a living for his family had done the best he could to provide each of the children with a suitable, inexpensive gift.

After having some refreshments, we had a word of prayer together, and then we walked out into the cold, crisp night. Though our feet were very cold, our hearts and souls were glowing with the warmth of that special family.

I have reflected upon that Christmas Eve on many, many occasions and have learned a number of lessons which my wife and I have tried to incorporate in our own family. One of these is that we can never judge the thoughts and intents of the heart of other people solely by their behavior. That night I saw in a family patriarch the seeds of godliness. I saw a son of God who, at least for a brief season, had overcome the temptations of the flesh and assumed his patriarchal role with dignity.

Second, I learned the great power of reading the scriptures as a family and vowed to do that when I married and had a family of my own. There is an important lesson to this effect at the very beginning of the Book of Mormon. The first chapter of that book recounts a vision beheld by Lehi in which an angel appeared to him and handed him a book, which he began to read, and "as he read, he was filled with the Spirit of the Lord." (1 Nephi 1:12.) From my experience in that tiny apartment in Germany in 1961, I learned that, even when our circumstances are not the best, when we read

the holy scriptures, the Spirit really does enter our homes and our hearts.

The third lesson I learned was that the great spirit of Christmas is available to one who has absolutely no interest whatsoever in commercial gifts. Because we, as missionaries, were on straitened budgets and this little family was also struggling financially, all of us focused our attention upon the gift of that little Babe in Bethlehem. There were no distractions.

This past Christmas my German wife, Dorothea, succeeded as she always does in bringing a special Christmas spirit into our home. We invited Grandma and Grandpa and one of our cousins to join with us and one of our daughters and our son in our Christmas Eve festivities. We sang the usual Christmas carols, which brought a wonderful spirit into our home, and then we read Luke 2 and briefly discussed the wondrous witnesses of the Savior's birth as outlined in Matthew 2. Various Old Testament prophets had prophesied that the Savior of the world would be born in Bethlehem (Matthew 2:6), that he would come out of Egypt (Matthew 2:15), and that he would be called a Nazarene (Matthew 2:23). We discussed how improbable that would have been in a day and age when people normally did not roam more than perhaps thirty miles from their birthplace. Yet the Savior was born in the opposite end of the kingdom from the place where he was reared as a boy. It would also have been highly improbable that someone would travel all the way to Egypt and even more improbable that he would return from Egypt to be called a

Nazarene. Nevertheless, all three of these prophecies were fulfilled, in keeping with the Lord's declaration that the truth will be established in the mouth of two or more witnesses (see Matthew 18:16).

When we finished our discussion of the events surrounding Jesus' birth, it was my wife's turn to tell us a Christmas story, and though we have celebrated thirty Christmases together, she has never told the same story twice. Each story is the capstone of our Christmas festivities.

As our little family Christmas service drew to a close, our daughter Stefanie exclaimed, "Opening presents just seems to be so anticlimactic at this point." All of us had felt the Spirit of the Lord, and Christmas gifts paled in comparison to the greatest Gift of all.

The Child in the Manger

ELDER MARVIN J. ASHTON

All my life I have had a special love for Jesus Christ. As a child I could relate to him. In my Primary days I can remember well asking my good mother to read to me about Jesus.

At Christmastime when I was a very young boy, when guests would drop in, my father would ask me to sing:

Away in a manger, no crib for his bed,
The little Lord Jesus laid down his sweet head . . .
I love thee, Lord Jesus; look down from the sky
And stay by my cradle till morning is nigh.
(Hymns, *no. 206.*)

Through the years it has remained my favorite Christmas carol, even though my father made me sing it when I would rather have not.

From Luke we read: "And she brought forth her firstborn son, and wrapped him in swaddling clothes, and laid him in a manger; because there was no room for them in the inn." (Luke 2:7.)

At Christmastime I am glad we refer to the birthplace of Jesus as a manger, but really it was a stable with conditions typical of any animal shed. There was

disorder, potential disease, infection, noise, whatever: hardly a suitable place for a child to be born. I think had there been room in the inn, there might have been a midwife or someone to help with the delivery, but as far as we know, Mary, with the support of her husband, took care of the birth on her own in those most difficult conditions.

I am so grateful that God, in his wisdom and for purposes best known to him, would make it necessary and even desirable for his only begotten Son to be born in a stable. Think of the significance of the greatest person ever to be born on earth starting life in a manger.

Yes, Jesus was born in a manger—in a stable. He came into this world as the son of Mary (inheriting from her the characteristics of mortality) and as the Son of Almighty God (inheriting from him the powers of immortality). He is the Firstborn of the Father. He gained the fulness of all things—he has all truth, all knowledge. He comprehends all and is infinite in all his attributes and powers.

He is the Son of our eternal Father and in due time will come again to reign with the righteous on earth. Under the Father he was chosen to work out the eternal Atonement and to put the whole plan of redemption, salvation, and exaltation into actuality.

My special witness, testimony, and declarations are prompted by the revelations of the Spirit. Jesus is our Savior, Redeemer, Messiah, and Friend. He lives. We know that as far as man is concerned, all things center in Jesus Christ.

Today Jesus stands at the citadel of our souls pleading for entrance. He pleads through the spoken word. He pleads through the scriptures. He pleads through the voice of the Spirit. He pleads through the voice of reason. He pleads through the witness of faithful parents and friends. But because we have no space left, we reply, "No room, no room." We have no room for Jesus because most of us are looking for a life of convenience, one that takes no time, costs no money, and requires no effort.

There is a sacred song that says, "I walked today where Jesus walked." Wouldn't it be thrilling if we could go and stand on that very spot of ground where Jesus stood and try to absorb the spirit of his life. Or suppose we could go

into Gethsemane and kneel at that place where under the burden of our sins he sweat great drops of blood at every pore. What if we went in our imaginations to stand before the final judgment bar? Then we might be able to more easily make up that list of things we could profitably get along without.

It may not be practical for us to walk today where Jesus walked. But it is practical—and a lot more important—to think today what Jesus thought. We can live today as Jesus lived. We can unload our hearts of evil and clear the lethargy out of our ambition. Then we can fill our minds with our Father's purpose, and our hearts with an understanding of his ways. We can loosen the latch and open the door of our souls and make room for the King of Glory to come in. To make room for our Redeemer is the greatest opportunity of our lives.

May the prayer of my favorite Christmas carol fill our hearts and be our desire at Christmas and always:

Be near me, Lord Jesus; I ask thee to stay
Close by me forever, and love me, I pray.
Bless all the dear children in thy tender care,
And fit us for heaven to live with thee there.
(Hymns, no. 206.)

The Joys of Christmas

PRESIDENT EZRA TAFT BENSON

I love Christmastime! And I find great joy in remembering Christmases past. Perhaps it is the emotion of the season that makes this time of year seem particularly poignant and meaningful and especially memorable.

Many events of almost nine decades of Christmases, dating back to my childhood on the Whitney, Idaho, farm where I was reared, are still clear in my mind. They are among some of the most enjoyable memories I have.

As a boy I loved going to the canyon to cut our Christmas tree, and I always tried to get one that reached to the ceiling. Though we received only a few gifts, our stockings were filled with fruit, nuts, and candy, and Santa always left something.

Like all children, we suffered terrible anticipation at Christmastime—until, that is, we happened onto the Santa Claus costume in the bottom of an old trunk. Suddenly the secret was out. So that was why Father was always out doing chores when Santa came on Christmas morning. The following December it occurred to me that if Father had been playing Santa

all those years, he and Mother must be hiding our gifts somewhere on the farm. I couldn't stifle my inquisitive mind, and in no time I'd led my younger brothers on a search that turned up several gifts buried in the wheat in the granary.

One of my favorite winter—and especially holiday—activities was taking out the big two-horse bobsleigh with bells on the horses. In those days, "Jingle Bells" was not only a song, it was a thrilling experience. There's nothing quite like riding through country lanes with the sleighbox filled with straw and a group of friends singing Christmas carols.

In Whitney on Christmas Day our family visited our grandparents, and we almost always traveled to their homes by bobsleigh. These were such happy occasions. Our grandparents were very musical and always provided entertainment of various kinds. There were recitations, skits, original poems, music, and dancing. Grandma Dunkley, a convert to the Church from Scotland, would dance the Highland Fling for us, and we loved that.

As with these recollections of childhood Christmases, warm memories fill my mind of the traditions Flora and I have enjoyed with our own family.

Our home was always decorated with holly and mistletoe and a beautiful tree. Flora and the girls baked delicious cakes and cookies—enough, it seemed at times, to feed a small army. One of our cherished Christmas possessions was a sturdy set of sleigh bells that had jingled each winter from Flora's father's cutter. When our chidren were young, we rang the bells outside their bedroom windows to signal that Santa Claus was coming. In later years we hung the bells on the front door, and the jingle when the door was opened brought back a parade of pleasant memories.

On Christmas Eve we would read together Luke's recounting of the Savior's birth, and sometimes Dickens' *A Christmas Carol* as well, and sing carols and hymns. Then, following the custom my parents observed when I was a boy, our children lined up a row of chairs, one for each child, and hung their stockings over the backs. Once the children were safely tucked in bed, Flora and I filled the stockings with candy, nuts, and fruit, and laid their gifts from Santa on and under their chairs.

I still remember those Christmas Eve nights when our youngest daughter crawled into bed with us in the middle of the night and tried to convince us it was time to get up. (I'll admit that at least once we gave in and let her take a peek at the tree and its treasures before coaxing her back to sleep.) But by five-thirty or so when we awoke to excited whispers and the sound of bare feet on the floor, we knew there was no keeping any of the

children in bed any longer. Soon we would shepherd them into the kitchen for a glass of milk and a roll. Then they would line up, youngest to oldest, and march into the living room. We loved their expressions of delight at their gifts.

Ours were really just ordinary Christmases—if peace and joy and togetherness can ever be called ordinary.

Flora always went to great lengths to make our home a wonderful place during the holidays. In the mid-1960s, when I was serving as mission president in Frankfurt, Germany, she returned from a visit to Salt Lake City with a suitcase full of frozen turkeys and cranberry sauce so that she could have a traditional holiday dinner for the missionaries. Truly, Flora has always radiated the spirit of Christmas.

In addition to warm memories about our family Christmas traditions and activities, my thoughts about Christmas past include a number of significant events that have taken place during the holiday season. The Decembers of 1945 and 1946, for example, will forever live in my memory. Just three days before Christmas in 1945, President George Albert Smith convened a special meeting of the First Presidency and the Council of the Twelve. With World War II finally over, President Smith announced it was time for the Church to reestablish contact with the Saints in Europe and distribute much-needed welfare supplies. In that meeting I was called to go to Europe as president of the European Mission to handle those assignments.

The call came as a complete surprise. Because of conditions in Europe, it was not possible to take my family with me. I had no idea what I would find when I got there, how I would arrange for travel throughout a continent that had been devastated by war, or how long the First Presidency would require me to stay. I was told that I should prepare to leave as soon as possible. This unexpected development affected greatly our preparations for Christmas and created an unusually sentimental and loving atmosphere in our home. Flora and I realized we would be separated for a period of time, and our feelings were tender at the prospect.

How grateful I was for her support, and for the knowledge we shared that this was the Lord's will for our family at this time. As the Christmas season drew to a close, I recorded in my journal: "The next year will no doubt be spent, in large measure and possibly in its entirety, abroad. It will mean some sacrifice of material comforts. I will miss my wife and sweet children and the association of the brethren and the visits to the stakes. I go, however, with no fear whatsoever, knowing that this is the Lord's work and that he will sustain me. I am grateful for the opportunity and deeply grateful that my wife, who is always most loyal, feels the same way. God bless them while I am away."

The following ten-and-a-half months were among the most challenging and yet rewarding I or my family had known. The separation tested our faith and endurance and physical energy to the limit, but helped us grow as never before.

I'll never forget the thrill of stepping off the airplane in Salt Lake City the following December, in 1946, and finding

Flora waiting for me. That Christmas was among the most poignant I have ever spent. Perhaps there had been no year in my life when my soul had been so stirred or when I had faced such challenges. I had been forced to rely completely upon the Lord, and my gratitude for his goodness and watchcare filled my soul and brought me easily to tears. I had come to love deeply the Saints in Europe, and leaving them had been a bittersweet experience.

But being home again brought such deep and fulfilling joy. Although the separation had been difficult for us all, we had grown even closer to one another. And as we realized how many blessings the Lord had given us throughout the year, tears flowed freely.

After the children had opened their presents on Christmas Day, I wrote in my journal, "The children were most happy and appreciative. There has not been an unkind word all day. In fact, we seldom hear arguments in our home. But this day has been especially blessed. It has been such a joy to sit with my angel wife and review the past, devoid of regrets, anticipate the future joyously, and count our many blessings gratefully. I shall never forget this glorious Christmas."

Of course, we have many other wonderful Christmas-related memories. Our family lived for eight years during the 1950s in Washington, D. C., while I served in the Cabinet of President Dwight D. Eisenhower. That unusual setting provided unusual experiences.

Almost every year we held a Christmas fireside in our home. Sometimes over a hundred young people crowded inside and sat on the floor, steps, or anywhere they could find a place. My wife and our daughters prepared wonderful refreshments for everyone, and I was honored to talk about the Savior and his divine mission. Some of these simple occasions brought greatest satisfaction.

Just four days before Christmas in 1954, our family had a special opportunity. President Eisenhower knew our custom of having a family hour one night during the week, and he expressed a wish to see how it was done. President and Mrs. Eisenhower and our family gathered that evening in the home of Bill and Allie Marriott for an evening of holiday fun and entertainment. Our sons performed comic skits and other readings, the girls sang, Flora recited a reading, and I did my part by leading the whole group in singing "John Brown's Baby Had a Cold upon Its Chest." It was plain, old-fashioned, homespun entertainment. The President and his party participated and seemed to enjoy it all; for our part, we were delighted to share the evening with them.

Another holiday season, some two decades later, brought an event of much different proportions. In 1973, after a very restful and contemplative Christmas Day, the following evening I received a phone call from President Spencer W. Kimball bringing me word of the sudden passing of President Harold B. Lee. President Lee and I had been boyhood friends dating back to our Idaho youth. We had even attended the same high school. I wrote in my journal, "It seemed impossible. He has been so well and I

have felt that he would be the last President of the Church I would know in mortal life. Some relief came as I knelt in prayer alone in my study, but I found it impossible to sleep until well after midnight."

Beyond my shock and deep sorrow for the loss of a dear friend was the realization that his death would have direct impact upon the course of my life. It was almost overwhelming to contemplate the possibility of my being called to serve as president of the Council of the Twelve. Perhaps one of the most telling aspects of that holiday season was the poignant realization of how completely I must rely on the Lord to help me do his will.

All of these Christmas memories, from the joyful to the sublime, from the excitement of opening packages to the serenity of tender reunions with loved ones, cause me to reflect on what Christmas really means and what impact the observance of the Savior's birth can have in our lives. Perhaps one of the greatest blessings of this wonderful Christmas season we celebrate is that it increases our sensitivity to things spiritual, to things of God. It causes us to contemplate our relationship with our Father and the degree of devotion we have for God.

It prompts us to be more tolerant and giving, more conscious of others, more generous and genuine, more filled with hope and charity and love—all Christlike attributes. No wonder the spirit of Christmas touches the hearts of people the world over: because, for at least a time, increased attention and devotion are turned toward our Lord and Savior, Jesus Christ.

This Christmas, as we reflect upon the wonderful memories of the past, let us resolve to give a most meaningful gift to the Lord. Let us give him our lives, our sacrifices. Those who do so will discover that he truly can make a lot more out of their lives than they can. Whoever will lose his life in the service of God will find eternal life.

Without Christ there would be no Christmas, and without Christ there can be no fulness of joy. It is my testimony that the Babe of Bethlehem, Jesus the Christ, is the one perfect Guide, the one perfect Example. Only by emulating him and adhering to his eternal truth can we realize peace on earth and good will toward all.

This chapter is excerpted from *President Ezra Taft Benson Remembers the Joys of Christmas*, Salt Lake City: Deseret Book, 1988.